GUIDEBOOK
TO
DISCIPLESHIP

_____

_____

_____

_____

GUIDEBOOK TO DISCIPLESHIP

Doug Hartman
and
Doug Sutherland

HARVEST HOUSE PUBLISHERS
Irvine, California 92714

Scripture quotations, unless otherwise indicated, are taken from the New American Standard Bible, and New Testament © 1960, 1962, 1963, 1968, 1971 The Lockman Foundation.

GUIDEBOOK TO DISCIPLESHIP

Copyright © 1976 Harvest House Publishers
Irvine, California 92714

Library of Congress Catalog Card Number: 76-20398
ISBN-0-89081-062-1

Foreword

Every sincere believer in Christ should be committed to the fulfillment of the Great Commission in this generation. We cannot be satisfied with business as usual. These are desperate times and only our total surrender to Christ is adequate to meet the challenge of this hour. Whoever you are, wherever you are, if you are available, God can use you—your time, your talents, your treasure—to help change this world. I believe that the greatest spiritual awakening since Pentecost is now taking place throughout the world and Christians everywhere have an unparalleled opportunity to become involved.

Our Lord said to His eleven men, "Go ye into all the world and make disciples of all nations." The only reasonable explanation for that command is that our

Lord did not expect these eleven men to accomplish this mission themselves. Obviously, He expected the Holy Spirit to accomplish this task through a strategy of discipleship. The result was a mighty spiritual awakening which changed the course of human history.

Campus Crusade for Christ International believes that the awakening of the first century will be duplicated in our time through the Church, the Body of Christ, under the direction and control of the Holy Spirit, as Christians win people to Christ, build them in the faith and send them out into a ministry of discipleship. Though our ministry is best known as a ministry that emphasizes evangelism, far more emphasis is placed on discipleship. Twenty-five years ago I realized that the vision that God had placed in my heart to help fulfill the Great Commission could never be accomplished through my own efforts whether in personal or mass evangelism. For this reason, our goal from the very beginning has been to disciple men who would in turn disciple others. Now a staff of some 5,000 is discipling tens of thousands who are in turn training and influencing millions more for our Savior. Nothing is more exciting or rewarding or consistent with the command of our Lord than making disciples for Christ and building disciplers of men.

Doug Hartman and Doug Sutherland have played a major role in helping to emphasize the importance of discipleship in our task. Thousands of lives have been influenced through their ministry. Thus, they have earned the right to write on this subject of discipleship. There is abundant tangible evidence of the effectiveness of this emphasis on discipleship in the lives of thousands of men and women who are investing their lives in helping to fulfill the Great Commission.

Jesus used a variety of methods and situations to build commitment into His disciples. It is evident that spending time with these men was a priority in His ministry. While He was evangelizing the multitudes, He was also giving special time and attention to His disciples. Our Lord knew well the necessity of developing faithful, committed men in order to see spiritual multiplication take place. It is from this perspective that *Guidebook for Discipleship* has been written.

Bill Bright
Campus Crusade for Christ International

_____

_____

_____

_____
_____

Introduction

After eight years of being involved in direct ministries of discipleship and seeing hundreds of individuals make decisions to enter full-time ministries, we have become aware of the tremendous need for God's church to understand the principles and perspectives necessary to build disciples today.

This concern led us to develop a week-end seminar, which we have conducted in every section of the United States and part of Canada. We have also had the opportunity to observe the results of these seminars as these individuals—pastors, Christian Organization staff, college students and church lay-people—applied what they learned to their own particular situations. The materials developed for these seminars form the basis of this book.

A Guidebook To Discipleship is not a standardized program of discipleship. It is instead a progression of workable dynamic principles of discipleship that can be employed in any existing church program. It is written to the church layman encouraging him to take advantage of the various church programs and activities in order to develop an exciting ministry of discipleship.

The book follows a simple four-part format: First, perspective preceeding his involvement; second, principles involving selection of his men; third, principles employed in the development of a disciple and fourth, an understanding of how a world-wide movement can develop through the local church.

A Guidebook To Discipleship encourages laymen to involve themselves in various discipleship programs— through its explanation of the principles and thinking behind the discipleship process. It also serves as excellent study material for discipleship groups. Furthermore, it aids church growth through assisting the pastor in communicating where the church is moving; aiding laymen in understanding how to use the church in their discipleship ministries; communicating to laymen the importance of the church and the importance of getting involved in church activities.

These concepts and principles are extremely versatile and can be utilized with any type of discipleship program which a church employs. Its versatility extends not only to existing discipleship programs but to different age groups as well.

Our thanks to Roberta Hartman, who along with her husband Doug, experimented with these principles over a period of years, and who wrote the materials used in the seminars.

Thanks also to Glenn Plate, who created the situation for the seminars—to Amy Hunt and Carolyn Brune, for their help with the manuscript—and to Ted Martin, for suggesting the book be written.

Doug Hartman
Doug Sutherland

Contents

PART III
DEVELOPMENT OF MULTIPLYING DISCIPLES

PART IV
DEVELOPING A MOVEMENT

PART I

BECOMING
A MULTIPLYING
DISCIPLE

_____

_____

_____

_____

1.

What's In It For Me?

"GO ... MAKE DISCIPLES!" With those exciting words, Jesus launched a movement that has changed the world. For three years, Jesus had poured His life into a few ordinary simple men. They were with Him when He stilled the sea, fed thousands from a boy's lunch, brought the dead back to life, and then rose from the dead Himself. He had told these simple men that they would do even greater things, and now, as Jesus left them with those words, they were on the move!

Through the power of the Holy Spirit, they healed the sick, brought life to those who were dead, and created such a stir of excitement throughout their world, that they were accused of "turning the world upside down" (Acts 17:6 KJV). What an exciting time to have been alive. Wouldn't it have been fantastic to have been one of those first followers of Jesus!

But the years have passed—hundreds of them. The movement marches on. It's now the twentieth century. Recently, a prominent atheist said, "If you Christians want us to think God has redeemed you, you had better start acting redeemed." It's easier for him to point out the problem than it is for Christians to work out the "how" of acting redeemed—especially in our messed-up world. Times have changed. Things have never been worse! You can't pick up a newspaper or turn on the TV without being bombarded with all the things that are wrong with our world. Crime is on the increase. In many parts of our country, divorces outnumber marriages. Wars are being fought, labor and management disputes are growing, poverty and economic problems seem to get worse instead of better.

Yet in many ways, our world is really not that different from the world of Jesus' day. Our problems seem more pressing partly because they are *our* problems, and partly because there are so many more of us. But the problems continue because men today use the same approach to problem-solving as they did at the time of Jesus. And they don't work any better today than they did then. Society must have its laws and the enforcement of those laws to protect people from themselves, but laws and law enforcement treat only the symptoms. The root of the problem is ignored—man's sinful heart. One can constrain evil men and make conditions somewhat better, but there is no law that can change a sinful heart.

Only radical surgery can get at the root of the problem—and that means a heart transplant. Jesus said, "I am the way, the truth and the life, no one comes to the Father but through me" (John 14:6). That's radical surgery. That's a new heart.

Man can make laws to try to control the symptom

but only Jesus Christ can transform man on the inside so that he becomes different on the outside—different with his relationships with people. He becomes a new creation, and a changed person equals a changed society.

The Christian is the only one who carries the innoculation for the disease of sin and God wants to use the lives of His children to change society. What a privilege to be involved in the task.

THE GREAT COMMISSION

A major theme of the Bible from *Genesis* through *Revelation* is that of reconciliation, bringing man back into a relationship with God. In Genesis God created man (Genesis 1:27) in a glorified state where he could have continued fellowship with God, the Father. Then in Genesis 3:6 man was tempted and sinned and fellowship with God was broken. From that point on the major theme through all of Scripture is that of restoring man to his original state where he has continual fellowship with the Father.

The Old Testament shows how God was preparing the world for His reconciling act. The Jewish people were selected by God to reveal the promises and prophecies of the coming Messiah, Who would die for the sins of all and make it possible for man to come back into a relationship with the Father. The New Testament explains God's plan to reconcile us and how He beckoned the world to accept the provision He had made. The Old Testament points forward to the Cross, while the New Testament points back to the Cross. The major theme of Scripture is reconciling a world separated from God by sin back into relationship with God (John 4:42).

In II Corinthians 5:17-19 Paul tells the Church at Corinth that "God was in Christ reconciling the world to Himself" and that the ministry of reconciliation was

17

given to the Church. One of the main purposes of the Church in today's world is to bring men and women to a saving knowledge of the Lord Jesus Christ. And the scope of that mission is nothing less than the world (Matthew 28:19, 20). This mission of reconciliation to the world is called the Great Commission. The amazing thing is that God is going to fulfill His Great Commission through people like you and me! It's exciting, but it's also the potential problem point.

PERSONAL CHARACTER DEVELOPMENT

The real problem in fulfilling the Great Commission is that God's people aren't experiencing the redeemed life. God has called us to a ministry of discipleship. As a person responds to this call, and develops as a disciple, and begins to disciple others, elements within his character begin to see dramatic transformation.

The development of character that occurs in the disciples' lives will also carry over and benefit such things as a person's occupation along with many other areas of his life.

In examining this character that results as an individual develops as a disciple we will see that spiritual maturity relates directly to the real world in which we live.

THE DEVELOPMENT OF
INNER CONFIDENCE

One of the greatest forces a believer faces today is that of peer pressure. Pressure from neighbors or friends which can cause them to lose their individual identity. There is pressure to do what the group does, go where they go, or else run the high risk of being an outsider or a loner.

When a disciple grows in his relationship with Christ, he has the potential of being freed from all this peer pressure. Instead of looking to a group of friends for fulfillment and trying to please them, he looks to Christ for the peace and fulfillment that He delivers. This fact allows the believer to really be himself. He does not have to conform to those around him because he is living for Jesus and not for his peers. He becomes what he was uniquely created to be—a real individual with a desire to please God.

When a person develops as a disciple and sees his life changing, he begins to see himself as an individual who is not afraid to stand for truth because he knows what truth is and that Jesus will not let him down. He begins to appreciate and accept himself for who he is. Why not? If Jesus can accept him with all his imperfections certainly he should be able to accept himself. And as he grows in the acceptance of himself, he gains greater emotional stability and becomes a more pleasant person to be around.

DEVELOPMENT OF LEADERSHIP

A disciple is a follower of Christ but he is also developing as a leader of men. There are at least two different kinds of leaders which individuals can become. There is the leader by position and there is the leader by influence.

An example of a leader by position might be an individual who graduates from a university and upon graduation receives a commission as Second Lieutenant in the United States Army. He goes through a two-month training program and then immediately takes command of a platoon of men. The men in the platoon are forced to follow that young leader because of the position that he holds. They do not have a choice; they must follow him. He is a leader by position.

An example of the second type of leader is Jesus. People followed Him because of who He was, because of His character and because He knew where He was going. The people did not *have* to follow Jesus but they *chose* to follow Him. He was a leader by influence.

As a person develops as a disciple, he develops in his relationship with God. As he develops in that relationship, he becomes more like Christ Himself. The Scriptures tell us that one of the purposes of the Holy Spirit is to conform us to the image of Christ (Romans 8:29). As the disciple is conformed to the image of Christ, he takes on more and more of His leadership style. Others will choose to follow him because of who he is, his developing character, and because he knows where he is going.

INCREASING IN WISDOM

Obviously, as a person develops as a disciple, he develops his relationship with God and learns more and more of the Scriptures. As an individual increases in knowledge of the Scriptures over a period of time, he gains a new perspective on life. He is not ruled by his five senses alone because he has a new basis for making decisions—the wisdom of God.

With wisdom comes direction. When a person makes decisions based on absolute truth, he has confidence that what he has decided to do is right. This inner confidence brings a feeling of purpose and self-esteem.

DEVELOPING A POSITIVE ATTITUDE IN LIFE

As a disciple learns to trust God's Word rather than be directed by the negative experiences around him, his general attitude gradually changes from negative to positive. This is because God's Word is positive. An individual walking in the power of the Holy Spirit is not plagued with constant worry, anxiety or deep depression, because he has given his life over to the Lord and now these problems are the Lord's problems. This frees up the child of God and can actually add years to his physical life, while at the same time make those "extra years" healthier years.

Medicine has shown that the state of mind of an individual affects his physical body. Anxiety causes ulcers and heart attacks, and worrying causes migraines and a host of other serious maladies. Therefore as one develops as a disciple, along with the constant encouragement of those with whom he is working, his new attitudes will become a positive force and may actually increase the length and quality of physical life.

CONCLUSION

In light of this chapter, it can be seen that a person's involvement in a ministry of discipleship will allow him to have a part in changing society, fulfilling the Great Commission while at the same time seeing the development of a personal Christ-like character.

ACTION

A person who develops a discipleship ministry benefits in a variety of different ways—not the least of which is the effective development of a strong and dynamic personal character. Personal character is the most important single ingredient for success in life, even by the world's standards.

As a person goes through life there are many things in which he could get involved and which would produce a certain amount of personal satisfaction. But there is nothing that even comes close to the personal satisfaction that can be obtained as he is involved in a ministry of discipleship.

The decision to be involved in this discipleship ministry could very well be one of the most important decisions you will ever make. Can you think of anywhere else where you could spend your time and get so much in return?

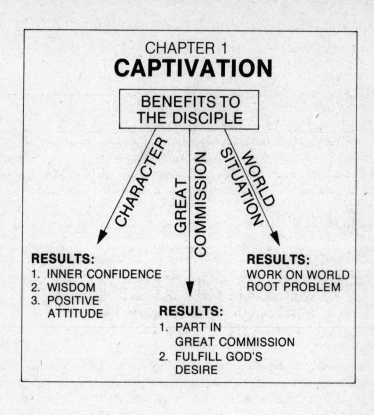

CHAPTER 1
CAPTIVATION

BENEFITS TO THE DISCIPLE

CHARACTER

GREAT COMMISSION

WORLD SITUATION

RESULTS:
1. INNER CONFIDENCE
2. WISDOM
3. POSITIVE ATTITUDE

RESULTS:
1. PART IN GREAT COMMISSION
2. FULFILL GOD'S DESIRE

RESULTS:
WORK ON WORLD ROOT PROBLEM

2.

What Kind Of Person Do I Have To Be?

As Jesus prepared His disciples in His final days with them, He emphasized many topics. One of them was what was necessary in order for God to work in and through their lives. Around that final supper table Jesus reminded them, "As the branch cannot bear fruit of itself, unless it abides in the vine, so neither can you, unless you abide in me" (John 15:4). Jesus made it clear that in order for God to work, certain ingredients were necessary. In order for God to produce the fruit mentioned in the first chapter certain characteristics must be at work in the layman's life.

The Apostle Paul certainly would be seen as one who experienced a Christ-like character and who had an impact on the world. What were the characteristics in his life as a disciple that made it possible for God to work in and through his life?

PAUL, ONE WITH A CHRIST-LIKE CHARACTER

One of the most important characteristics in Paul's life was his heart for God. From the moment of his conversion on the road to Damascus until his death many years later he sought to be in fellowship with his Lord. Sitting in prison he wrote to the believers in Philippi, "I count all things to be loss in view of the surpassing value of knowing Christ Jesus my Lord, for whom I have suffered the loss of all things, and count them but rubbish in order that I may gain Christ" (Philippians 3:8). This heart for God made it possible for God to do so much in his life.

Paul was a brilliant man—a leader of the Pharisees. He was educated under Gamaliel. He was probably a good businessman. However, he knew that his strength as a disciple of Christ was dependent upon the inner working of the Holy Spirit. Paul wrote to the Romans "But if the Spirit of Him who raised Jesus from the dead dwells in you, He who raised Christ Jesus from the dead will also give life to your mortal bodies through His Spirit who indwells you" (Romans 8:11). It was only through dependence on the Holy Spirit that Paul experienced the benefits of being a disciple.

Another key characteristic in the life of Paul was that he was teachable. He sought truth in the word of God. He revealed this aspect of his life when he wrote to Timothy "Be diligent to present yourselves approved to God as a workman who does not need to be ashamed, handling accurately the word of truth" (II Timothy 2:15). Paul constantly was bombarded with influences that tried to divert him or may have tempted him, but he never lost sight of his objective. The reason was he evaluated them in light of his objective—which was to bring God glory through his life. Paul wrote "Run in such a way that you may win. Therefore I run in such a way, as not without aim; I box in such a way as not beating the air" (I Cor. 9:24, 26). He always evaluated his activities in the light of his objective. The individual involved in a ministry of discipleship must learn to relate all things to his objective.

Through the letters Paul wrote, it becomes obvious that Paul had many friends. He loved those with whom he worked and he loved to be with them. Conversely people loved to be with him. They would travel many miles to minister to him or just to be with him. Paul was able to demonstrate his love by making friends. This is a vital characteristic to the believer in Christ who aspires to be a disciple and a discipler of others.

PAUL, THE METHOD OF HIS MINISTRY

Along with experiencing the fruit of God's *working in his life,* Paul also saw God use him mightily to make an *impact on the world.* What was the method God gave Paul to use? Because of the importance of this method, the rest of this book will develop and explain it.

Paul's method to reach the world is found in his letter to Timothy. In II Timothy 2:2, Paul tells Timothy to take the things which he has heard from Paul and teach them to faithful men who will in turn teach others also. This is the familiar geometric progression of numbers. In other words, Paul's method of discipleship to reach the world was through the process of multiplication.

To see the significance of the multiplication method a contrast will be drawn with another approach. This second approach seems to be the way most Christians think the world will be reached. In this approach the individual has as his actual objective, the world of 4,500,000,000 people. He believes the best way that he can reach his objective is by speaking to as many people as possible about the claims of Christ. He devises a plan by which he will speak to 1,000 people a day and each group of 1,000 people will be different. In order to accomplish this, he has organized a group of helpers to go into a community, organize the publicity and other details, so that when he arrives in the area all he has to do is preach. The results are fantastic. As a matter of fact, the results are so fantastic that he does not take any days off. This individual goes on and on preaching to 1,000 different people every day throughout the year. At this rate, it is only going to take him 10,958 years to reach the world, assuming of course there is no population growth.

In contrast to this approach, the multiplication method would be characterized as follows. An individual, living in an average community shares Christ with his neighbors and friends until he finds three who want to develop in their faith and become multiplying disciples. He now works with these three for an entire year, teaching them how to share their faith and then taking them out and letting them try it. He teaches them how to feed themselves from the Word and how to teach others to feed themselves. These three have a vision and philosophy. They want their lives to be involved in a ministry of multiplication. After a year's time, these three go out and each find three others in which they reproduce their lives, now there are nine. In another year the number grows to 27 as each of those nine find and build three others. At the end of four years there are 81; 5 years—243; 6 years—729; 7 years—2,187; 8 years—6,561; 9 years—19,683; 10 years—59,049; 11 years—177,147; 12 years—531,441; 13 years—1,594,323; 14 years—4,782,969; 15 years—14,782,907; 16 years—43,046,721; 17 years—129,140,163; 18 years—387,420,489; 19 years—

1,162,261,467; 20 years—3,486,784,401; 21 years—10,460,353,203.

Through the multiplication method, the world could be totally discipled (not just exposed to the Gospel) in 20 years, starting with just one individual.

It is important to realize that this example may seem a little idealistic. God works uniquely in each individual's life making it impossible to program reproduction in neat one-year segments. However, the example does point to a very important fact. If one wants his life to have a significant impact for God, he will want to be involved in multiplication. It is easy to see now why Paul's method of discipleship was multiplication.

Notice also, in II Timothy 2:2, that Timothy was "in the presence of *many* witnesses" and that he was to entrust what he was taught "to faithful men." This implies that it was in groups that successive leaders of other groups were developed. In other words, the multiplication of groups of *leaders* was Paul's method.

In diagramming this multiplication method of discipleship it would be something like this:

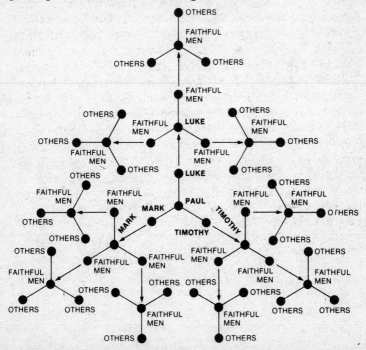

In the rest of this book the disciple who is multiplying in this method of discipleship will be called a "multiplying disciple." We will use this term so as to distinguish him from the variety of other definitions given to the term "disciple." Also, using "multiplying disciple" will underscore the method of discipleship employed by this particular kind of disciple.

ACTION

1. There are at least five characteristics, in the life of Paul, which a man or woman of God must have to develop a discipleship ministry. Can you list them?

2. The apostle Paul never seemed to lose sight of his ministry goal. There was that constant desire and drive to present the gospel to every human being in the world. Are you able to describe his method in detail?

3. Can you explain the difference between a "disciple" and a "multiplying disciple"?

CHAPTER 2

OBSERVATION

CHARACTER OF THE MAN

1. PHILIPPIANS 3:8	1. HEART FOR GOD
2. ROMANS 8:11	2. RELIED ON THE HOLY SPIRIT
3. II TIMOTHY 2:15	3. TEACHABLE
4. I CORINTHIANS 9:24, 26	4. KNEW HIS OBJECTIVE
5. II TIMOTHY 4:19-21	5. BUILT RELATIONSHIPS

HIS METHOD

II TIMOTHY 2:2	MULTIPLICATION

_____

_____

_____

_____

3.

TERMINAL THINKING VS. RELATIONAL THINKING

In Robert Coleman's book *Master Plan of Evangelism*, he writes: "His (Jesus') life was ordered by His objective. Everything He did and said was a part of the whole pattern. It had significance because it contributed to the ultimate purpose of His life in redeeming the world for God. This was the motivating vision governing His behavior. His steps were ordered by it. Mark it well. Not for one moment did Jesus lose sight of His goal."

The person who has become a multiplying disciple thinks in a way which is not necessarily common to our particular culture or educational systems. He thinks in a "relational" manner rather than in a "terminal" style. "Relational" thinking is defined as the process of relating activities and knowledge to an objective. "Terminal" thinking is defined as the process whereby activity and knowledge are objectives and ends within themselves.

TERMINAL THINKING

Terminal thinking occurs when the individual involved does not relate his knowledge or activity to any ultimate objective.

When the average individual starts to school at the age of five or six, he is taught to think in a particular manner—"terminally." In grade school, he learns that if he wants to go from the fourth grade to the fifth grade, he needs to be able to do what the teacher wants him to do. When the average person goes to high school or to college he learns that in order to get a good grade, he needs to remember what the professor said in class and be able to give back exactly the same thing on a test. He really does not have to understand the far-reaching purpose for anything he is learning. When the individual graduates and is ready to start making his own way in the world, he has already been conditioned to think in a terminal manner. He does not relate the activities in which he is involved on a daily basis to any objective, he just does them.

Picture in your mind a teenager. He walks outside one night, possibly during the summer, looks up at the stars and asks that age old question of himself, "What is my purpose for being here anyway?" ... And he really could not come up with a good answer. Perhaps his parents are Christians who have led exemplary lives and told him about God's plan for his life from the time he was a small child. But he still doesn't experience the reality of the purpose for his life. So, what he does is put the question in the back of his mind and go on with the business of living. As a result his life is directed by the activities in which he is involved.

This is like the fellow who was very busy digging a hole in the ground. He really did not understand why he was digging the hole but as long as he kept busy digging, he did not have time to think about it. He felt he was accomplishing something. After all, people said that he was, and in his daily schedule he was always busy. But exactly what it was that he was trying to accomplish in the long run, he didn't know.

In the average local church there are many who attend church services, go to Sunday School, sing in a choir and even come to all the church business meetings. They carry a full load of church activities but never really consider how these activities are helping to accomplish their own individual purpose for life. They do not *relate* what they are doing to their ultimate objectives. Perhaps they do not even realize that there is any ultimate purpose for their life. These people are solid church members, leaders of the local community, and well educated in the Scriptures. They perhaps are able to relate portions of Scripture to specific situations which face them everyday, but they are examples of terminal thinkers because they do not relate their activities to their ultimate purpose in life.

RELATIONAL THINKING

Relational thinking occurs when an individual relates knowledge and activities to an objective in his life.

To understand relational thinking, picture an individual who, after finishing his undergraduate study, became involved in full-time Christian work. As he was involved in his particular ministry he started to understand the fantastic significance of relating everything that he was doing to his ultimate purpose which was to "give God glory." Now he had been aware for quite some time that man's ultimate purpose in life was to give God glory, but it seemed to be more of an academic understanding. He studied the Word, gave his life in a total way to the Lord, was involved in full-time Christian service, yet there was still something missing. He was using the same terminal thinking style he had been conditioned to use when he was in school. He had been conditioned to think in terms of immediate results rather than to think "relationally," i.e. relating·everything he did to his ultimate purpose in life.

He became excited about "relational" thinking and since he was ministering on a college campus at the time, he began to ask university students what they felt their ultimate purpose in life was. He would strike up a conversation with an unsuspecting student and gradually turn the conversation. He would ask questions such as "Why did you come here to the university?" The answers he would get were often times comical—answers like, "I came to college because I didn't know what else to do," or "My parents expect me to go to college and they are paying the bill." He would then ask, "But why do you go to class, what is your objective?" The student would usually answer, "If you want to get good grades you gotta go to class." He would ask, "Is that your purpose for life—to get good grades?" The student would usually get kind of indignant at this point and respond, "Of course not, (pause) if you want to graduate you gotta get good grades." "Is that your purpose in life, to graduate?" The student, now getting a little nervous, "You gotta graduate in order to get a good job, to give security to your wife, so you can have cute kids." "Is that your reason for existence, your ultimate purpose—to have cute kids?" The student—"Listen, I would like to talk some more but I gotta go to class."

This illustrates that most individuals do not think in terms of their ultimate purpose for life. They think terminally rather than relationally because that is the way they have been taught to think.

As one begins to think relationally rather than terminally he will become more and more aware of the fantastic power and life-changing potential which can be realized by the application of this truth. He will see how an individual who learns to think relationally, can reach extremely high levels of commitment and accomplish tremendous feats of achievement. Secular men have taken this truth, which was intended to be used by the believer, and used it to make money or to gain a position of power.

As a person develops as a multiplying-disciple he will start to develop a style of thinking which is common to great leaders.

THE CONCENTRATION PRINCIPLE

While developing relational thinking, the multiplying disciple will also want to take advantage of another powerful principle. This is the concentration principle and is defined as "whatever captures a man's mind captures him and becomes his true objective."

The story of Steve illustrates the concentration principle. One day, after a campus Bible study, Steve came up to the Bible study leader to ask if it would be possible to talk further about a problem he was having. The leader suggested getting a cup of coffee at the union, but Steve wanted to discuss the problem in a more private surrounding. So he invited the leader up to his dorm room. On the way to the room, Steve talked about how he became a Christian in his local church several years ago and that during that time, he had studied the Bible and had tried to have a consistent time of prayer. Steve, speaking a little more softly, said that even though he had been a Christian for

34

some time, he was still having a terrible time trying to control his lust. He really wanted God to give him victory in this area. He prayed about it but things seemed to get worse rather than better. They talked a little more and then arrived at Steve's room. Steve unlocked the door and held it open so the leader could walk in. When they got inside the leader looked around the room and could hardly believe his eyes. All over Steve's bulletin board were pictures of the Playboy bunny of the month. The walls of the room were papered with pictures of nude models. Even the ceiling had pictures posted on it! The Bible study leader turned to Steve and said, "I think I might have an answer for you concerning your problem of lust."

In this situation, Steve was constantly focusing his mind on pictures of nude models. The result was that he was actually programming his mind to become more and more plagued by the problem of lust.

The Bible study leader explained to Steve how our minds can be programmed, and how God gave us a will so that we could freely decide what will fill our minds. He continued to explain that God wants us to focus our attention on Christ and that the result would be that we would be transformed into His image.

From this illustration it can be seen that the concentration principle is always in operation. It is operating in your life whether or not you are aware of it. And it is one of the most powerful principles that will ever affect a person's life. The person who is developing as a multiplying-disciple uses this dynamic principle in the context of his relational thinking style, which he is developing in the power of the Holy Spirit.

TRANSFORMATION

When the multiplying disciple understands how the Holy Spirit works in his life to give him power to live the Christian life, and understands how to think relationally, the concentration principle comes into play. The result is that the multiplying disciple is not being conformed to this world but is being transformed by a renewing of his mind.

There was a young man who was doing well in a business which he had started. He was invited to a conference not fully understanding what he was attending. The speaker spoke of a personal relationship with Christ and how each person must make their own decision. This young businessman bowed his head and asked Christ to come into his life. As time went on, he grew in his new faith but felt more and more that God was calling him into the ministry. So he tried to keep his business running while he went to seminary. It was while he was at seminary that God revealed to this man the purpose for his life. That purpose was to see the Great Commission fulfilled in his generation. From that moment on, this man evaluated everything he did in terms of how it was going to help accomplish his purpose. He thought relationally.

He would evaluate what he ate. He stayed away from certain foods and ate a special diet. He felt that if he ate the wrong things it would cause him to lose strength and he would not be as effective in accomplishing his purpose.

He evaluated what he did. Once this man was in attendance at a conference with other Christian leaders. They were planning to go skiing after the conference ended and he decided he would go. Then he learned that it was dangerous to ski if you have never been skiing before and that many people break their legs. He re-evaluated the activity in terms of his purpose, and decided that the possibility of spending two months in a cast would slow him down too much and make him less effective in accomplishing his purpose.

This man was just an average person that God was using in a dynamic way because of his faithfulness to Him and his relational mind-set. God has used this man to bring literally millions to a saving knowledge of the Lord in every free country of the world. He is a leader among leaders whom God continues to bless. God has blessed not only this man but his wife and family also. A finer, more loving, family would be hard to find.

This man first of all understood the power of the Holy Spirit—that it was the Holy Spirit's power and not his own determination that accomplished those intermediate goals which led to his ultimate purpose. He believed God and had the faith that God would be true to His Word.

Secondly, this man continued to employ a thinking style like Jesus'. His ultimate purpose was the motivating force in his life—everything he did, he did in accordance with his ultimate purpose—even his eating and drinking (I Corinthians 10:31).

Thirdly, this man, because of his relational thinking style allowed the concentration principle to work *for* him instead of against him. As he evaluated every activity in light of how it would be used to accomplish his purpose, the Great Commission occupied more and more of his mind's time. As the Great Commission occupied more of his mind's time, he became more and more "captured" by his purpose.

The result was that this man was totally motivated by his purpose. He had an unbelievable vision for how God can work in our society and a large faith to believe God for that vision. He was a compassionate, understanding man, totally committed to his purpose.

ACTION

God can use you in a dynamic way also, but one of the first things to do is to start to develop the proper mind-set or thinking pattern.

1. The first thing you need to do is to determine your ultimate purpose. May I suggest "The glory of God."

2. Define the activities in your specific situation in terms of the purpose for your life.

   —For example, if you were married one of the ways that you would glorify God would be to maintain and develop a good marriage. Don't be too detailed at first, keep it simple and the Lord will add to your understanding. Simply ask the question, "Is what I am doing glorifying God?" and "Could I be doing something different that will glorify God more?"

3. Three times a day consciously evaluate your activities in terms of your ultimate purpose. The meal times are a natural.

   —At breakfast consider the activities to be done that day and evaluate them.

   —At lunch evaluate what you have done and what you are doing at the present time.

   —At dinner evaluate what you have done that day and make plans for tomorrow.

Don't be discouraged as you start if you find it difficult. This merely indicates that you have been conditioned to think terminally over many years, so it is going to take some time to establish a new habit pattern of thought.

It is not necessary to establish the relational habit pattern of thought before starting this discipleship program. The program is designed to continually encourage you to think relationally as you go through it so that as you develop a multiplying ministry, you will also be developing a powerful relational thinking style that God will use in unbelievable ways.

CHAPTER 3
PERSPECTIVE

SHORT RANGE		LONG RANGE
NOT CREATIVE		CREATIVE
MAN-PLEASER		GOD-PLEASER
	TERMINAL THINKING	
CONTROLLED BY CIRCUMSTANCES		NOT CONTROLLED BY CIRCUMSTANCES
	RELATIONAL THINKING	
DOESN'T RELATE ACTIVITIES		RELATES ACTIVITIES TO PURPOSE
FLUCTUATING SELF-IMAGE		STRONG SELF-IMAGE
CONTROLLED BY PROGRAM		USES PROGRAM

_____

_____

_____

_____

4.

HOW DO I ORGANIZE MY LIFE?

The story is told of a young businessman in the mid-West. He was a very dedicated Christian and wanted his life to count for the Lord. The only problem was that his business seemed to take up all of his time. But he went to church every Sunday and was head of the ushers. However, he just couldn't find time to do much more in the way of a ministry, even though he desired it. One day a Christian friend challenged him to make a schedule. He was to divide each of the seven days of the week into 24-hour slots. He then listed the non-negotiable elements in his life such as working, eating, sleeping, etc. He followed with the next most necessary activities. When he had finished his schedule he was amazed at the time left over. He saw that a lot of his time was going to activities that were not an asset to his life. As a consequence, he began a ministry of multiplication in the lives of some fellow church members with all this newly discovered free time.

This story is an illustration of the need for anyone who desires to be a multiplying disciple to have his life organized. In order for the multiplying disciple to employ relational thinking he must know if and when different elements of his life fit into his purpose.

PURPOSE FOR LIFE

Before the multiplying disciple can relate things to his purpose he must know what his purpose for life is. Genesis 1:27 tells us that man was created in God's image. If man is to reflect the image of God then he must radiate the glory of God. Isaiah 43:7 says, "Everyone who is called by My name, and whom I have created for My glory...." In other words, we were created for God's glory. These two references, along with many others, tell the Christian that his purpose in life is to glorify God. This becomes the rudder of his life. He relates all his involvement in life to this purpose.

RELATIONSHIP WITH GOD AND MINISTRY

The most logical question that comes to the believer's mind after knowing his purpose is, how do I glorify God? The scriptures seem to group the answers to that question into two areas. They are, first, to develop his relationship with God and second, to develop his ministry. In Matthew 22:37, Jesus told the questioning lawyer that to love the Lord with all his heart, soul and mind was the greatest commandment and the second was like it, love your neighbor as yourself. This dualism to glorify God can also be illustrated by the

Psalms and the Proverbs. Psalms is the record of those who were developing a relationship with God while Proverbs is about those who wanted to develop wisdom to minister in other people's lives.

Even though these two channels to glorify God are separated they are not mutually exclusive. They are interdependent and must be in balance. One cannot glorify God in his ministry if he is not walking with God and one cannot walk with God unless he is having a ministry. This is seen in John 21:15-17 when Jesus asked Simon Peter, "Do you love Me? Then feed my sheep."

These two ways to glorify God are also seen as Jesus chose His disciples. Mark 3:14 says, "And He appointed twelve, that they might be *with Him* and that He might *send them out to preach.*" One can also note the interdependence between the two methods when it says that *"He* might send them out to preach."

In light of this, the multiplying disciple has as his ultimate purpose in life to glorify God. He does this through developing his relationship with God and by developing his ministry.

OBJECTIVE, POWER, METHOD

Within each of these divisions there is an objective, there is the power to do them, and there is a method. The objective of one's relationship with God is to reach full stature in Christ (Eph. 4:13). The power to accomplish this objective is the Holy Spirit. The method is through developing in all areas of one's life: spiritual, physical, social and mental. These four areas are also interdependent with each other.

In the area of developing one's ministry, the objective of this ministry is the world (Mark 16:15). The power is the Holy Spirit and the method is by multiplication through the multiplying disciple (II Tim. 2:2).

It is important to note that the word "purpose" is

used to indicate the ultimate for the Christian, while "objective" is used to describe subsidiary goals within that ultimate purpose.

The multiplying disciple's life is now organized so that he can apply relational thinking. Without organizing every facet of his life into this purpose, he is vulnerable to terminal thinking.

As an illustration, the multiplying-disciple evaluates the books he reads under the category of "mental," which is under the "method" of "developing his relationship with God"—which is one of the two areas in which he "glorifies God." He evaluates his business responsibilities under the area of social, and relates it to the glorification of God via his relationship with God.

In the area of developing his ministry, the multiplying disciple knows that the way he will reach his ministry objective of the world is to employ the method of multiplication. Therefore he will center his ministry on the development of the multiplying-disciple. For every church activity he asks the question, "how will this help the development of my multiplying-disciples?"

The rest of this book is devoted to helping you be a multiplying-disciple and to develop the ministry of multiplication so that you can have an impact on the world for Christ.

CHAPTER 4
PURPOSE

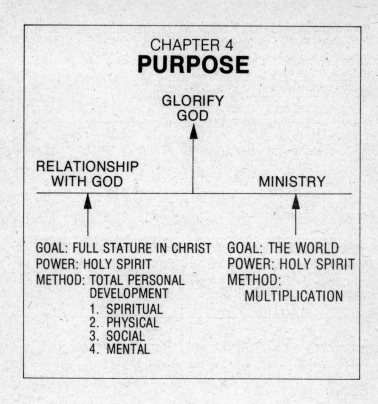

GLORIFY
GOD

RELATIONSHIP
WITH GOD

MINISTRY

GOAL: FULL STATURE IN CHRIST
POWER: HOLY SPIRIT
METHOD: TOTAL PERSONAL
      DEVELOPMENT
    1. SPIRITUAL
    2. PHYSICAL
    3. SOCIAL
    4. MENTAL

GOAL: THE WORLD
POWER: HOLY SPIRIT
METHOD:
    MULTIPLICATION

_____

_____

_____

_____
_____

PART II

SELECTION OF THE MULTIPLYING DISCIPLES

Now that the layman has seen what God can do in and through his life, the need for him to develop relational thinking and how to organize his life to bring God the most glory, he is ready to begin his ministry of developing multiplying disciples to go to the world. The question that comes to his mind at this point is where and how do I begin to select these men? Jesus, followed by the disciples and the apostle Paul, paved the way for the multiplying disciples of today to know where and how to select the right people.

The selection process of the multiplying disciple will be developed in this section by first showing that selection comes out of a following; second, that an environment is used to prepare the believer for selection; third, that the environment is not only for selection but is also the place where the body functions together; fourth, how to identify potential multiplying disciples; and fifth, how to challenge the potential multiplying disciple.

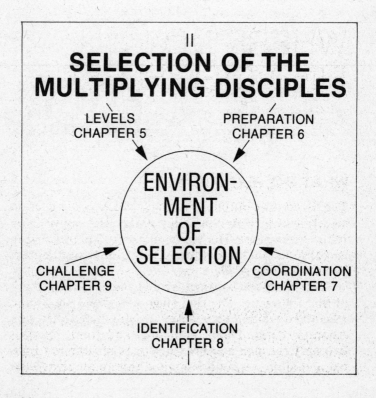

II
SELECTION OF THE MULTIPLYING DISCIPLES

LEVELS
CHAPTER 5

PREPARATION
CHAPTER 6

ENVIRON-
MENT
OF
SELECTION

CHALLENGE
CHAPTER 9

COORDINATION
CHAPTER 7

IDENTIFICATION
CHAPTER 8

_____

_____

_____

_____

5.

WHERE DO I
FIND DISCIPLES?

WHAT DID JESUS DO?

The Scriptures outline a method which Jesus used in selecting the twelve apostles. After His baptism by John, Jesus began His public ministry. He traveled in and around Galilee and the city of Capernaum gathering a following as He went.

There were four distinguishable stages in the growth of that following. The first stage was made up of men who were waiting to believe. This included men like Andrew, Peter, Philip, Nathaniel and John. At least two of these men had been disciples of John the Baptist and all five were hungry and thirsty for righteousness (John 1:43-51). They had been primed by John and were ready to accept Jesus as their Messiah.

The second stage is distinguishable by the fact that men believed on Him. John called Jesus "The Lamb of God who takes away the sin of the world" (John 1:29). It appears that at least the first five disciples recognized Him and now believed on Him as their Messiah.

The third stage is when the disciples were occasional companions of the Master. They would, of course, learn from his teaching but the level of involvement is not comparable to the fourth stage.

The fourth stage of following was characterized by constant and continued association with Jesus. They were taught but they were also exposed to a variety of ministry situations. You could say they were being trained for ministry in a group situation. They had not yet been chosen to be the twelve as this would take place later on. There is a new level of commitment demonstrated at this stage. This is where personal sacrifice began to emerge as a few of the followers abandoned, at least in part, their secular occupations.

These four stages called the "four-staged following," are seen in the group following Jesus before he selected those who he was going to develop as multiplying disciples. Out of this four-staged following He selected 12 men to be multiplying disciples.

VIEWING THE CHURCH ACTIVITIES

The average person may already be involved in all types of church activities. Therefore, how can he even begin to think in terms of establishing a four-staged following from which to select those he will disciple? The answer is so obvious that it is often overlooked: organize the activities in which he is already involved according to various stages of involvement. This may involve a re-evaluation of his activities and what these activities are actually accomplishing in relation to his objective. (Development of *relational* thinking is continually encouraged throughout the entire discipleship process.) The result may be that the layman will drop a few activities and pick up others in their place.

SELECTING
THE MULTIPLYING DISCIPLE

Stages of Involvement
Stage 1—Pool of Humanity
Stage 2—Evangelistic Activities
Stage 3—Bible Study
Stage 4—Training

STAGE 1—POOL OF HUMANITY

The first stage in Jesus' following was made up of men who were wanting to believe on Him. Some did and some did not. This stage provides a place for all of those who for one reason or another have not accepted Christ into their lives or who are not personally interested in your program.

In a local church situation, this stage includes all of those individuals who have had at least some contact with the church or the Gospel. It includes activities which might be labeled pre-evangelistic, such as Boy Scout meetings sponsored by the church or social gatherings of all sorts. The "Pool of Humanity" stage also represents all of those individuals who have attended, at one time or another, a church service or a church function. Usually these people filled out a "visitor's card" and the church has kept a record of who they are. Finally, stage 1 could be represented by all those people who have heard the gospel from members of the congregation, either in a formal way—church visitation team—or an informal way over a cup of coffee or at work.

STAGE 2—EVANGELISTIC ACTIVITIES

The second stage in Jesus' ministry is distinguishable by the fact that these men did believe on Him.

The purpose of this stage in the local church is to continually provide a series of activities designed to present the claims of Christ and give people a chance to respond. It also provides meetings in which one can participate, but for one reason or another, has no desire to move into a higher stage of involvement.

Stage 2, or the Evangelistic Activity stage, could be represented by the Sunday morning church service, by a special Sunday school class designed for those wanting to start a relationship with Christ, or an evangelistic Saturday morning men's breakfast. The evangelistic outreach stage could be represented by visitation teams or any meeting which would give the participant a chance to receive Christ.

For example, Jim was a local building contractor in town. He had always been a good man but for some reason had never been able to make it to church. Bill invited Jim to come to a Saturday morning men's breakfast at the church. Jim really did not want to go, but Bill said that he would buy the breakfast. Since they worked on Saturdays anyway, Jim had to eat breakfast somewhere.

When they got to the church, Jim noticed that many of the other men were dressed in their work clothes too and that made him feel a little more at ease. At breakfast, everyone was friendly and asked him questions about the construction business. After breakfast one of the men got up and gave a short five minute witness for Christ, sharing the Gospel and giving all of those there a chance to pray and ask Christ to come into their lives. Jim bowed his head and asked Christ to come into his life. He really had enjoyed the meeting, the food was hot and he could not beat the price.

Jim was continually encouraged to become involved

in higher stages of involvement in the church, but the only thing Jim wanted to do was go to the Saturday men's breakfast. He attended the breakfast for more than two years and became rather close friends with some of the other men during that time. Finally, after two years of observing in the other men a quality of life he wanted and did not have, he accepted a standing invitation to participate in one of the men's home Bible studies. Jim was now on his way to participating in higher stages of involvement. Jim is a good illustration of the purpose of Stage 2.

STAGE 3—THE BIBLE STUDY

The purpose for this stage of involvement is to provide a bridge to the stage of training. Stage 3 is characterized by Bible teaching as compared to evangelism in Stage 2.

The "Bible study stage" could be represented by church services which are primarily teaching in emphasis. The Sunday school could also be used to build people in the Word. Home Bible studies are another facet of this level, as is any activity which is aimed at developing an individual through the Word and bringing him to a higher stage of involvement.

As an illustration of how stage 3 would function we use the story of Bob and Jane. They had attended church and Sunday school ever since they had married a year earlier. They noticed that more and more people in the church were talking about becoming multiplying disciples. The pastor would make reference to it from the pulpit every once in a while and the whole church seemed to have a new sense of direction. However, they had other things which occupied most of their free time. It was all they could do to make it to church and Sunday school.

The Sunday school teacher had been teaching the book of Romans and kept emphasizing the need for personal training. He continually explained how man's whole purpose was to glorify God and that one of the ways a person can do that is by leading others to Christ. He explained the importance of putting God first in one's life. He also explained that it may require a little sacrifice but would in the long run be very profitable.

Bob and Jane, after being exposed to this type of encouragement for several months, started to feel a personal need for some training. They also started to realize that it was entirely possible that a few of their priorities were out of line. After discussing this together and praying for direction, Bob and Jane decided to make time to attend the training classes at the church.

Bob and Jane were occasional attenders in the "Bible study stage of involvement." The Sunday school class which they attended was geared to prepare and encourage them to advance to the higher level. There was no pressure put on them. They were welcome in the Sunday school level for as long as they wanted to attend but they were constantly encouraged to commit more of their lives to Christ.

STAGE 4—THE TRAINING LEVEL

The purpose for the training stage is to equip the saints for service by training them in elementary concepts of how to share their faith, walk in the power of the Holy Spirit, follow-up an individual after they respond to the gospel and generally learn what is involved in a multiplying ministry before actually beginning one.

Another purpose of this stage of involvement is to expose the people to a variety of ministry situations, such as visitation teams, leading small groups, teaching Sunday school and organizing a fellowship dinner so they can start to determine what their spiritual gifts are. The idea is to train everyone in the basics of sharing their faith and follow-up, to encourage them to find a suitable area to serve and to constantly emphasize the dynamic potential in developing a multiplying ministry.

The "training stage" in many local churches is represented by an ongoing program at a regular time. Other churches really do not have any special activity designed especially to train its people. If this is the case, there might be some thought given to starting a series of classes designed to train individuals in a group situation. There are many programs available. One of the most effective training programs is offered by Campus Crusade for Christ and called the "Way of Life Plan."

Dr. Sam, and his wife Betty, are representative of the fourth stage. They had attended church regularly, taught Sunday School and had even talked privately of going into full-time Christian service. They had never really had a peace, however, about selling their home and pulling their children out of school in order to go to seminary. After all, God had given Sam a tremendous skill as a doctor and they both thought he should use it. But there was still that tremendous desire to demonstrate their commitment to God. Teaching Sunday School was fine but they felt they ought to be doing more. They did not know what that "more" might be but they did know they were too busy just to fill their time up with "more" activity. They wanted their time to really count.

Their church started offering training classes in how to walk in the power of the Holy Spirit, share their faith and learn basic concepts of discipleship. Dr. Sam and Betty enrolled right away. The classes lasted for thirteen weeks and during that time Sam and Betty had a chance to put into practice in their neighborhood what they were learning in class. God worked in their lives and they started to understand how they could have a significant ministry without leaving home.

When the classes were over they were asked if they wanted to go on and learn to be multiplying disciples, continue in the training stage by helping teach the classes or serve in some other area of the church. Sam and Betty talked about it and prayed about it for quite awhile before making their decision. They decided they wanted to develop a multiplying ministry. This was a very big decision for them because they realized that it would take a lot of their time—time which they could be giving to other worthwhile things. But they knew they were doing the right thing. This was a once in a lifetime opportunity for Sam and Betty and the answer to their prayers. They could have a dynamic ministry right where they were. After Sam and Betty accepted the challenge, God gave them His peace. They felt like they were a young couple again ready to start life all over. They knew it was going to be difficult but the "pros" far outweighed the "cons." God had finally given them a way to demonstrate their commitment to Him in a dynamic, significant way. They were prepared to be selected and start development as multiplying disciples.

ACTION

1. Evaluate the church activities in which you are involved in light of these four stages of involvement. Select the ones which best meet your needs and accomplish your purpose.
2. Encourage and challenge other individuals to move up and through the four stage following.

Remember you are not just thinking in terms of individual activities but instead you are seeking to use the activities to help you accomplish a personal objective that God has given you.

As you start to view your activities not merely as an end in themselves but as the means to an end, your involvement begins to have a greater sense of purpose.

CHAPTER 5
LEVELS

LEVELS OF INVOLVEMENT	DEFINITION	EXAMPLE OF CHURCH ACTIVITY
1	POOL OF HUMANITY	BOY SCOUTS SOCIAL GATHERING
2	EVANGELISTIC ACTIVITY	SUNDAY SERMON VISITATION
3	BIBLE STUDY	SUNDAY SCHOOL HOME BIBLE STUDY
4	TRAINING	TRAINING CLASS

SELECTION

_____

_____

_____

_____

6.

CREATING THE ENVIRONMENT FOR DISCIPLESHIP

As one moves through the four stages of involvement described in Chapter 5, there is an important element in this movement. That element is the freedom to make your own decision as to your stage of involvement.

WHAT DID JESUS DO?

Jesus was aware of this element as He selected His men. As He traveled through the cities of Galilee and Judea, He would continually challenge men to follow

Him. But He didn't force a man to follow Him who, by an act of His own will, decided not to do so. In Luke 18:18-23, Jesus challenged the rich young ruler to give all that he had to the poor and to follow Him. The rich young ruler, after considering the cost, decided not to follow Him. Then there was the man Jesus challenged to follow Him. He responded by saying yes but that first he must bury his father (Luke 9:59). Jesus replied by saying, "Let the dead bury the dead." The man decided by an act of his own will, not to follow Jesus but to bury his father.

There was even a man who accepted Jesus' challenge to follow him and then after following Him for awhile, decided by an act of his own will not only to quit following Him but to also betray Him. This, of course, was Judas.

Jesus, in selecting His following, allowed men to make their own decisions. When some decided not to follow Him, He did not plead with them to change their minds. He encouraged men to exercise their own will by challenging them to make a decision. Today, as men are presented with the claims of Christ, they are the ones who must decide if they want to commit their lives to Him. Another person cannot make that decision for them—they must exercise their own free will.

FORCING AN INDIVIDUAL

Just as Jesus allowed an individual the freedom to choose his level of commitment, the discipler should maintain this kind of freedom. He should never force an individual into a commitment who is not prepared by the Holy Spirit to be committed to a higher level of involvement. Results of this kind of pressure could cause frustration or possibly push an individual further from the Lord. Instead, the discipler should be sensitive to his disciple's specific level of commitment and increase opportunities for involvement by an attitude of encouragement and challenge—not "pushiness." The discipler should tell his disciple to let the Lord direct him and then honor the Holy Spirit's work in that individual's life.

CREATING AN ENVIRONMENT

The main thrust of the four-staged following is to create an environment where the people can select the program that best meets their needs.

In the four-staged following, an environment is created where the individual, in much the same manner as the Biblical examples, is encouraged to make his own decisions as to what he wants to do. Of course counsel is provided, but the individual is allowed, under the influence of the Holy Spirit, to decide for himself. After an individual has had a chance to assess what his needs and desires are, he then makes the decision as to what level in the four-stages of involvement would be best for him. When that has been determined, he makes other decisions such as what activities or programs he will take advantage of in his selected stage.

This whole concept encourages the individual to develop a relational thinking style, making decisions in relation to their own personal objectives. One of the results is that the person involved becomes much more a part of the activity they choose. It causes them to look at the activity not merely as an activity but as a key step to meet their goals. It possibly could lead to other activities of a higher stage of involvement.

THE SEA SHELL

In many ways the four-staged following is like a shell which one would find on the shore of the sea. A shell is a hard and cold structure. The only element that makes the shell part of a living organism is the sea creature which lives inside of it. This tiny sea creature uses the shell so it can function more effectively and carry out the purposes of its life. The shell is only important as it benefits the sea creature. It has no life, in and of itself. The shell does not use the sea creature—the sea creature uses the shell.

The four-staged following is like that sea shell in that the Holy Spirit is the one who gives the life and makes the structure part of a living organism. In allowing the Holy Spirit to work, the individual is encouraged to trust Him and make his own decisions. The result is that those involved in the structure move through the progressive stages of involvement at varying rates of speed. Some individuals might stay in the outreach stage for as long as a year and then move quickly to the training stage. Others would move through the stages of involvement as the Holy Spirit worked in their lives, at more of a regular, steady rate. Still others would move steadily up to the training stage and then drop down to the "pool of humanity" stage for awhile before moving back up again.

IMPORTANCE OF CHALLENGING

In setting up the four-staged following, the idea is to create an environment for the Holy Spirit to use and not to try to use the Holy Spirit to complete a particular discipleship program. As one uses the four-staged following, the success of building multiplying disciples is totally dependent on the ministry of the Holy Spirit in the believer's life. If the Holy Spirit does not work in the believer's life and cause him to make his own decisions to become more involved, then he doesn't move through the four-staged following and he is not selected to be a multiplying disciple.

This does not mean, however, that there is no need for challenging or encouraging others to higher stages of involvement. On the contrary, Paul perhaps understanding the sovereignty of God and the working of the Holy Spirit better than anyone else "urged" fellow believers to a higher level of commitment (Romans 12:1-2). In II Timothy 4, Paul challenged Timothy to a dedicated ministry. It is very important to continually challenge and encourage those in the following to move to a higher level of commitment. In fact, if those in the four-staged following are not constantly challenged and encouraged, the people could very easily become content where they are—causing the following to stagnate.

As the four-staged following is implemented and the purpose for each stage is emphasized, certain types of individuals will filter themselves out. In a very real sense, it is God who is selecting the individuals who will be developed as multiplying disciples. They will be challenged to start developing as multiplying disciples.

In many ways, selecting a potential multiplying disciple consists of first setting up the four-staged following and making sure that it becomes an environment that the Holy Spirit can work through. Second, challenge and encourage individuals to move through it, and third, select the ones God has raised up.

HOLDING STRUCTURE

The idea of creating a four-staged following, which would be an environment, would tend to work against specific time limits which an individual must fulfill in order to move up in the stages of involvement. The four-staged following becomes a holding structure. If people do not feel ready to move closer to becoming a multiplying disciple, they can stay at the level they wish until the Holy Spirit causes them to exercise their will and make a decision to move to another stage. This could mean that an individual will stay at one stage for a month, a year, or for the rest of their life.

AN EXAMPLE

There was a couple who were approximately 45 years old and who were located in stage 1. They visited the church once after they had first moved into the community but they had not been back for two years. Recently, a couple from the church visited with them and shared effectively how they could know Christ in a personal way. The husband and wife, after asking several questions, both prayed to ask Christ to come into their lives. The couple from the church then invited them to a small informal Bible study in their home. The new Christian couple met in the informal study group for two months and during that time developed a good relationship with the church couple. They were continually being invited in a subtle way to attend church but the invitation was always ignored. Finally, after months of growing in the Word and developing a good relationship with the church couple, they started attending Sunday School and church. The couple was now at stage 3 or the Bible study stage. (They skipped over stage 2 and went directly to stage 3.)

They continued to attend church and their Bible study. They were continually encouraged to start in the training classes on how to share their faith but they did not feel that they were ready.

While they were at stage 3, they enrolled in a series of special programs in the church. Some of the programs lasted two weeks while some lasted a couple of months. After each program, those attending were encouraged to start the new training classes in stage 4 but this couple would just get involved in another stage 3 study program.

Finally, after one year in stage 3, they decided to take the training classes which lasted 13 weeks. After the training classes ended they were seriously trying to decide if they should drop back into stage 3 for more Bible study and less commitment or start training as a multiplying disciple—stage 4.

In this illustration, God worked uniquely in the lives of this couple, allowing them to make up their own minds as to what stage of involvement they wanted. This couple was allowed to move through the various stages at their own rate as the Holy Spirit worked in their lives. Even though the emphasis here is on the Holy Spirit raising an individual at His own rate, there is also a continued emphasis placed on challenging and encouraging.

ACTION

1. Since this strategy depends so much on the person of the Holy Spirit, it would be helpful to go through and study a series of booklets published by Campus Crusade for Christ entitled the "Transferable Concepts."
2. As individuals move through the four stages, encourage them but do not push. Think through how you might continually encourage someone. Remember to be tolerable and trust God in people's lives.
3. Look and pray continually for the one God raises up for you to work with and develop as a multiplying disciple. Many times it is a person you would least expect. Look at the twelve Jesus picked. Would you have picked them?

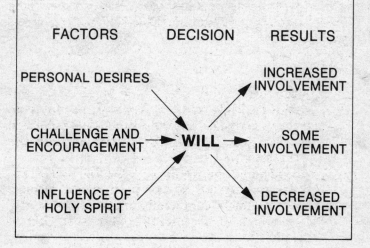

CHAPTER 6
DECISION CONCERNING AN INDIVIDUAL'S INVOLVEMENT

FACTORS   DECISION   RESULTS

PERSONAL DESIRES   INCREASED
                                    INVOLVEMENT

CHALLENGE AND   WILL   SOME
ENCOURAGEMENT   INVOLVEMENT

INFLUENCE OF   DECREASED
HOLY SPIRIT   INVOLVEMENT

_____

_____

_____

_____
_____

7.

WE REALLY NEED EACH OTHER

It is important that, as the multiplying disciple uses the four-stage following to select his men that he also understands that it serves another purpose. That other purpose is to provide a place for the body of Christ to function together as described in I Corinthians 12.

PAUL'S LETTER

Paul, in his first epistle to the Corinthians, writes to a church situation where the members of the congregation were beset with a number of serious problems. Paul starts his letter by informing the Corinthians of their heritage in Christ, "In everything you were enriched in Him'' (I Corinthians 1:5). Then Paul continues sighting specific problems in the church and giving instruction for proper church conduct. Then in chapter 12, Paul expands on the area of spiritual gifts.

Paul emphasizes that all believers belong to the same body but that the body has many members (I Corinthians 12:13). He goes on to say that the members of the body are also different (I Corinthians 12:13) but that they are still members of the same body (I Corinthians 12:16). Paul also stresses the point that even though believers are different from one another and that they do different things, they still need one another (I Corinthians 12:21-22). This point is amplified by Paul who writes that those individuals who seem to be unimportant and accomplishing insignificant things could actually be those upon which are "bestowed more abundant honor." God is the one who has given us all our special abilities and our uniquenesses and He has placed us in the body just as He desired (I Corinthians 12:18).

This passage illustrates the second purpose for the four-staged following. The first purpose was discussed in the previous chapters—creating an environment from which potential multiplying-disciples can be selected. The second purpose of creating a four-staged following is to provide an environment for everyone in the body of Christ to be involved in a meaningful way, that they would be involved in such a way as to encourage them to develop their full potential in order to glorify God.

THE MEMBERS OF THE BODY ARE DIFFERENT

God has created each individual with His own unique blueprint, just the way He desired. Each person is different from every other person in the world. Each has his own personal set of needs, hopes and desires.

Many times, however, when an individual is developing in his faith, some more mature Christians expect him to develop the exact same way they developed in their faith. If they do not see the same patterns of growth occurring in their brother's life, they are tempted to ask him why he is not growing. The truth of the matter is that he is growing, but he is growing in his own unique way.

There were two friends, Bob and Al, who both lived in the same neighborhood and worked at the same job. They were printers for a national magazine. Bob and Al spent a lot of time together because they had a lot of the same interests.

One day when they were at work, a mutual friend came by and asked if one of them would take his son to the church's annual baseball banquet. His son was really looking forward to it but he was going to be out of town. Al said that he would go since he played ball when he was a kid.

On the way home, Bob and Al stopped at the same bar where they always stopped for their usual after-work drink. It was in the bar that Al started to express to Bob the apprehension that he was starting to feel concerning the baseball banquet at the church. Neither Al or Bob had been to church since high school—fifteen years ago. Bob told Al that if it would make him feel better, he would go to the banquet with him. Al really seemed relieved and the conversation then took a lighter tone as they joked about the events of the day. They kidded each other about being fat since they were both about forty pounds overweight. Then they headed for home.

Three days later Bob and Al picked up the boy and took him to the church's baseball banquet. It was a good dinner and Bob and Al enjoyed the free tickets. Then something happened that they did not expect. There was a special speaker—a visiting missionary. Bob and Al looked at one another and gave a silent sigh. The missionary told of some experiences he had on the field and then he gave a clear presentation of the Gospel. Bob and Al had both been listening intently to the missionary and were ready to make a decision and commit their lives to Christ. The chance came at the end of the banquet. The missionary closed in prayer and asked those who wished to receive Christ for the first time to raise their hand.

The next day, Bob and Al started to read some of the material that they had picked up in the church lobby. It was not long before they started reading the Bible and attending church regularly.

Then one day as they were working in the shop, Bob asked Al if he had still been reading the Bible. Al said yes and then Bob said, "If you still read the Bible then why do you still drink beer when we go to the football games? That was one of the first things God cleared up in my life." Al felt a little defensive; he had no idea that Bob felt he was insincere about his faith because he still drank beer. Then Al responded, "Why are you still forty pounds overweight? That was one of the first things that God took care of in my life!"

Bob and Al started to experience the first big strain in their friendship in five years and it was all because they did not understand that God worked uniquely in each individual's life. In Al's life, God worked on the weight first before He convicted him of drinking. In Bob's life, God worked on the drinking first.

Individuals who are using the four-staged following are tempted many times to view those in higher stages as more spiritual or more mature than those in lower levels. This is against the philosophy of the four-staged following. The philosophy of the four-stage following is to provide an environment that the Holy Spirit can use any way He wants to. It just might be that God is working in a very profound way in the lives of individuals in the lower stage. The idea of the four-staged following is not to rank individuals in levels of spiritual maturity but to provide an environment where individuals who have a variety of needs can be ministered to.

JUDGING SPIRITUALITY

Another of the major principles which is important is that of not judging the spirituality of those who may not be interested yet in developing as multiplying disciples. Through this whole process of selection, an individual comes in contact with a wide variety of personal ambitions and aspirations. Because one person might be convinced that the best way for him to glorify God is to become a multiplying disciple he might infer that it is the best way for everyone else to glorify God. This may or may not be true. Again, individuals are created by God unique beings with unique combinations of strengths and weaknesses. It is very unlikely that one person can understand how God is going to work in everyone else's life. Therefore, it is difficult to judge a man's spirituality based on how his activities compare to someone else's. When an individual is involved in the selection of a multiplying disciple, it is important to not infer that everyone who chooses not to have a multiplying ministry is less spiritual.

NEED FOR ONE ANOTHER

Another principle emphasized in I Corinthians 12 that is applied in the four stage following is our need for one another. There was a ministry situation where there were several individuals who were all preparing to be multiplying disciples. They were all having a good ministry and God continued to teach each of them many things. But there was one problem. As they prepared their individual multiplying ministries, an attitude of competition started to emerge. Sally started to find fault with Jerry because he was such a disciplinarian and overlooked many of the personal needs of those with whom he worked. On the other hand, Jerry was having a great ministry; God used his personal discipline to encourage others to greater works. Jerry reacted to Sally's charges of insensitivity and said that Sally was so sensitive that none of the women she was working with had any backbone. Jerry felt that they were all "wishy-washy." Sally, interestingly enough, was having just as good a ministry as Jerry. Her women were just as committed to the Lord as Jerry's men and they were all starting to develop ministries of their own.

Finally, Jerry and Sally got together and started to talk things out. They each listed their strengths and their weaknesses on a piece of paper. The Lord gave them the realization that one gift is just as spiritual as another. They were just different. Jerry and Sally also came to the realization that they both had weaknesses. They saw that if they worked together instead of in competition with one another, God could bless their efforts even in a greater way. They saw that they needed one another to have an effective ministry.

This attitude between Jerry and Sally gave them a real understanding of how the body of Christ can work together and grow in love. Jerry and Sally started to really appreciate each other for who they were instead of complaining about who they were not. This same type of coordination takes place in the four stage following.

EVERYONE CAN HAVE A PART

Another principle in I Corinthians 12 that is contained within the four-stage following is that every part of Christ's body is needed in multiplication. Tom was a faithful and sincere Christian who had served the Lord in various ways for many years. Tom wanted to become a multiplying disciple because he felt that was how he could have the most strategic ministry for the Lord. He would wake up every morning and pray for the ones that he could develop and build as multiplying disciples, but no one seemed to want to work with him. He had some personal habits that were kind of unusual and people just tended to stay away from him. Tom studied the Bible, read books on discipleship but still could not establish a ministry.

Then one day Tom got interested in Christian literature. The pastor asked Tom to introduce a few new books to part of the congregation during a weekend retreat. Tom did. Later, some of those who bought the books came up to him and told him how much they had helped. Tom was encouraged and decided to buy a small bookstore in order to help other members of the congregation. He would review the books and tell members of the congregation how they could increase their ministries if they used certain books. The bookstore grew and grew. God greatly blessed this man's faithfulness. Years later Tom was supporting a dozen overseas missionaries with the profits from his bookstore. He had contributed new books to the church library and a healthy tithe to the church treasury. Tom was having a ministry through his bookstore which enabled others to develop as multiplying disciples. Tom was having a ministry which contributed to multiplication without actually being a multiplying disciple himself. This points to a very important element in the four-stage following, namely, that even those not *directly* involved in the discipleship process are necessary for it to come to fruition.

SUMMARY

The four-stage following allows for different types of individuals to develop as multiplying disciples exercising their unique gifts. Jerry and Sally were different but they accomplished the same thing. The only difference was they accomplished it in a different way.

The four-stage following also allows individuals who have gifts and interests which would not lend themselves directly to becoming multiplying disciples to still develop their gift (like Tom's bookstore) and contribute to a multiplying ministry.

ACTION

1. Recognize that not everyone is like you and that God may deal with their life differently than He did with yours. If you have been judging someone, make things right with that person.
2. Continue to pray for God to raise up the ones He has for you to work with.
3. Start to consider how you might use the strengths of others in your church, such as your Sunday School teacher or your choir leader, to assist you in building multiplying disciples.

CHAPTER 7
COORDINATION

FOUR STAGE
FOLLOWING

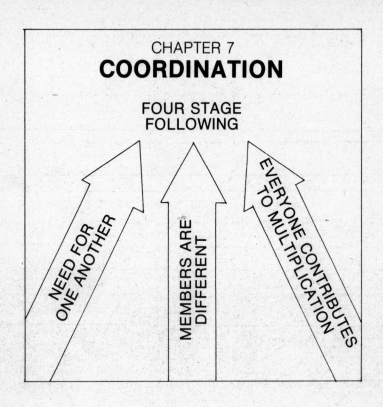

NEED FOR
ONE ANOTHER

MEMBERS ARE
DIFFERENT

EVERYONE CONTRIBUTES
TO MULTIPLICATION

_____

_____

_____

_____
_____

8.

How Do I Know
Who To Select?

The United States Marines have a recruiting slogan that says they are looking for a few good men. The characteristics of the man God uses are different than the United States Marines standards. But He does have qualifications. The extent to which the multiplying disciple's ministry grows is dependent upon the quality of person selected. Therefore, identification of those whom God wants to raise up is very important to the multiplying disciple. Jesus took great care in selecting the eleven men out of multitudes of disciples. He looked for qualities that the world would term foolish. Yet, His selection was correct because every Christian today is a testimony to the faithfulness of those men.

In Chapter 2 we listed five characteristics in Paul that made him God's prototype of a multiplying disciple. It is these same qualities that the multiplying disciple is looking for as he begins the selection of his men. These qualities will not be re-defined in this chapter. Instead, we will consider the way you can identify those qualities in an individual.

Before Jesus selected His disciples, Luke 6:12-13 says, "It was at this time that He went off to the mountain to pray and He spent the whole night in prayer to God, and when day came, He called His disciples to Him; and chose twelve of them, whom He also named as apostles." God is the one who raises up and puts down, therefore it is God who brings the multiplying disciple's men to the forefront. Prayer cannot be minimized in the identification of the multiplying disciple.

HEART FOR GOD

The first quality that we saw in Paul's life was his heart for God. One will never make it as a multiplying disciple if he doesn't seek the Lord with all his heart. This quality is manifested by noticing what it is that the individual talks about—Does he center most of his conversation around His Lord? Also, if he has a heart for God he will relate the decisions in his life around what would be glorifying God.

Many a person has the outward appearance of a Christian leader but if he doesn't have a heart for God he won't last long. This is the characteristic that pro-tects him from being diverted from his mission.

DEPENDENCE ON THE HOLY SPIRIT

Jesus told the disciples, "you shall receive power when the Holy Spirit has come upon you; and you shall be my witnesses both in Jerusalem, and in all Judea and Samaria, and even to the remotest part of the earth" (Acts 1:8). The potential multiplying disciple must demonstrate a dependence upon the Holy Spirit. The whole multiplication process outlined in this book is dependent upon having an environment for the Holy Spirit to work.

A dependence upon the Holy Spirit is manifested by the fruit of the Spirit (Gal. 5:22-23) in the individual's life. Does he demonstrate faith in light of hard circumstances. Does he get upset when things don't go as he had planned? These are a few ways that one can tell if he is depending upon the Holy Spirit or not.

TEACHABLE ATTITUDE

Proverbs says that one cannot be taught unless he wants to learn. To develop as a multiplying disciple, an individual must want to learn.

A teachable attitude comes forth by noticing if the individual asks a lot of questions about the Word of God and about how to be more effective in his ministry. He also demonstrates a humble spirit. Is he always sharing the new things he is learning?

BUILDS RELATIONSHIPS

A very important characteristic in the multiplication method of discipleship is that of building relationships. It is so important that if an individual cannot build strong relationships he cannot be involved in the method of discipleship outlined in this book.

There are several questions to ask concerning the potential multiplying disciple in this area. Does he have many close friends? Do people like to be around him? Does he like to be around people? Does he give without expecting in return? The key word in this characteristic is "give." Does he give of himself to others?

RELATIONAL THINKER

The final characteristic to look for in a potential multiplying disciple is does he relate all that he does back to the purpose of his life (chapter 3). The question here is does he know where he is going?

This factor in one's life is demonstrated by the fact that he uses the activities in which he is involved to help him reach his objective. He knows what he wants to do with his life. His life is organized. He can say "no" to things and does not just flow with the crowd. God's multiplying disciple knows where he is going.

SUMMARY

The potential multiplying disciple doesn't have to be great by the worlds standards, but he must have a heart for God, a teachable attitude, depend upon the Holy Spirit, be able to make friends, and be a relational thinker. God can work through a man like this to "turn the world upside down."

ACTION POINTS

1. Apply some of the questions in this chapter to your own life to see areas of development needed in your life to be a multiplying disciple.
2. Begin to take these five characteristics and look for them in the people in your church.

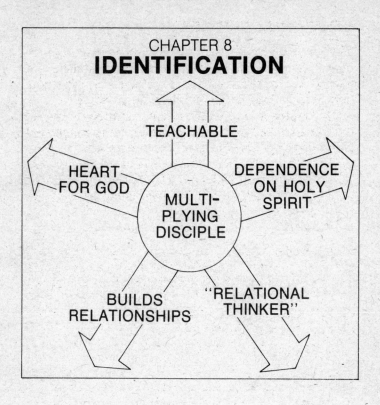

CHAPTER 8
IDENTIFICATION

TEACHABLE

HEART FOR GOD

DEPENDENCE ON HOLY SPIRIT

MULTI-PLYING DISCIPLE

BUILDS RELATIONSHIPS

"RELATIONAL THINKER"

_____

_____

_____

_____

9.

How Do I Enflame Their Hearts?

In the previous chapters, some principles have been discussed regarding the various procedures involved in selecting a multiplying disciple. But what is actually involved in approaching a potential multiplying disciple?

Jesus was the one man in history who continually challenged individuals throughout His earthly ministry. He challenged the disciples to leave their nets and follow Him (Matt. 4:20). He challenged the rich young ruler to sell all he had and give it to the poor (Luke 18:18-23) and He challenged His disciples to go and make disciples of all nations (Matt. 28:19, 20). Even today Jesus challenges men to follow him.

HE KNEW THEIR NEED

Much of Jesus' ministry was characterized by not only filling the spiritual needs of people but also by meeting their physical needs. He healed the sick, gave sight to the blind, and cured the leper.

Jesus also related spiritual significance to the meeting of physical needs. For example, after He had cast out the demons in a man who was blind and deaf, Jesus related spiritual truth to His followers (Matt. 12:22-28).

In challenging an individual to become a multiplying disciple, it is important to show how the accomplishment of spiritual objectives will relate to the basic needs of an individual. His needs are met through two areas of his life: First, by developing his relationship with God and second, by developing his ministry. As an individual develops in his own personal relationship with God he will have the true desires of his heart fulfilled (Ps. 37:4). As this relationship develops the individual starts to become more conformed to the image of Christ resulting in various changes which begin to appear, such as:

1. The development of inner confidence.
2. Development of a leader possessing wisdom and common sense.
3. Development of a positive attitude in life.

These are just a few examples of how developing a relationship with God can relate to basic needs a man or woman might have.

As an individual develops his multiplying ministry, he will also have certain basic needs met. One of which is the need to have his life really count for something—to somehow be used to influence other lives for good. When an individual develops a multiplying ministry, he is working with the most valuable asset the world has to offer, and in the most significant way.

Therefore his self-worth rises.

It is very important, in the first part of the challenge to the potential multiplying disciple, that he sees the benefits of his involvement in a multiplying ministry. These benefits infiltrate every area of his life.

COUNTING THE COST

To follow Jesus means personal sacrifice. He told His disciples to drop their nets and to follow Him (Matt. 4:20). In another situation, He implied that we must be prepared to abandon everything if need be for the sake of the Gospel (Mark 10:29). In becoming a multiplying disciple the individual has to know it is going to cost something in order to receive the benefits of developing a relationship with God and having a multiplying ministry. It is going to cost time. The old adage goes "You get what you pay for." In a very real sense, his time can represent his money. He must decide where he is going to spend his time, and compare that to what he is going to get in return. The individual who invests his time in the discipleship program, which is being offered to him, is in for the bargain of his life. He needs to see that. He needs to realize that what you are offering him is more important to him than any of his other options.

He needs to see that you are not asking him to just be involved in more activities that will take up his time, but that every activity is especially designed to accomplish one of the two objectives. Those objectives are his objectives and he is being offered the most effective way to accomplish them.

THE SPECIAL ACTIVITIES

At this point it might be good to explain the required special activities and to give the reasons why they exist. These special activities are the standards that are necessary to develop one as a multiplying disciple.

There are three general reasons why there are certain required activities.

The first reason is because it allows people of like-mind to be together. If an individual really wants to accomplish the objectives of establishing a relationship with God and a multiplying ministry, the activities will act as a filter and screen out those who do not have the same objectives. This is important because two people who have different objectives will never agree on the same method to reach those respective objectives. A person who really wants to accomplish a certain goal wants others around him who have the same desire.

The second reason these activities are important is because it will help maintain a balance in the developing multiplying disciple's life. This balance is between personal growth (developing a relationship with God) and training (developing a multiplying ministry) as was discussed in Chapter 3.

The third reason is to establish favorable habit patterns in the multiplying disciple's life. These habit patterns are patterns the individuals might wish that he had but as of yet he has not developed them. An example of this might be sharing his faith as a way-of-life. This is a habit pattern he wants to develop and one of the purposes of the special activities is to assist him in establishing these habit patterns.

Here are a few examples of the special activities in which a multiplying disciple might be involved:

1. Sharing his faith regularly.
    a. Regular sharing is important because it helps to keep the individual fresh in his walk with Christ. Therefore, it helps in developing his relationship with God.
    b. Regular sharing provides a source of individuals for the individual to involve in the four-staged following and eventually his multiplying ministry. Therefore, it helps in ac-

complishing his ministry objective.
  c. Regular sharing gives the individual a chance to train those he is discipling so again it relates to developing a ministry.
2. Conducting his own Bible Study could also be an example of a special activity.
  a. Having a Bible Study provides a place to continue working with those with which the individual has shared. Therefore, it relates to his ministry.
  b. A person who teaches a Bible Study always learns more than those he teaches so it aids in an individual's spiritual knowledge. Therefore, it relates to developing his relationship with God.
  c. A Bible Study serves as a good position from which the individual can challenge others to a multiplying ministry.
  d. Having a Bible Study helps give the individual experience in leading a small group. That experience will be very important as he challenges men to a multiplying ministry. Therefore, it relates to his developing a ministry.
  e. Having a Bible Study puts the individual in a place where he must trust God. Therefore, it relates to his personal growth.
3. Attending the group meeting where he is being developed as a multiplying disciple (this will be developed in Chapter 11).
  a. The purpose of this meeting is to train one on how to develop a multiplying ministry.
  b. The second purpose of this group is to help him develop his relationship with God.

The individual uses the special activities to help him accomplish his personal objectives. They are not just activities in which he is involved but are used as a means to an end. (Relational thinking continually is encouraged.)

FOLLOW THROUGH

After Jesus selected and challenged His disciples, He committed Himself to them. Jesus would spend more and more time with them as the cross grew closer. He loved His disciples and they loved Him. It is important for the one challenging the individual to commit himself to those he has challenged. The following story offers a good example of how a man found and selected a disciple and then how he committed himself to him.

Dean was looking and praying for the one which God would raise up for him to work with and develop as a multiplying disciple. He would share his faith and would go to group meetings in his church. Then one day he decided to start a Bible Study in his home. Dean invited a few friends to come and he served coffee and doughnuts in an informal atmosphere. The Bible study lasted for several months and during that time, he observed the others in the group. He looked for that one who might be interested in developing as a multiplying disciple. Finally, Dean challenged one of the men in the group. He explained how developing a relationship with God and a personal multiplying ministry could really be exciting and how it could meet basic needs in his life. He explained the time commitment and the special activities, being very careful to show the purpose behind every activity.

The man thought for a minute and then asked if he could go home and pray about the decision for a week. He was quite busy and it would mean some extra time commitments. The next week he returned to the Bible Study, pulled Dean aside and told him that he had decided to commit himself to become a multiplying disciple. From that point on, Dean made his friend his first priority. The Bible Study was fun but now the Bible Study was viewed as helping build his first multiplying disciple. Dean and his multiplying disciple became the best of friends as they developed their multiplying~ministries together.

SUMMARY

It is very important to share the vision before the time commitment or the special activities. Before an individual will commit himself to any program, he needs to see how it will help him accomplish his personal objectives. When a person begins to see the discipleship process as a means which he can use to glorify God and accomplish his personal objectives then the required special activities are viewed as valuable assets. If, on the other hand, a person does not understand that he is to use the discipleship process rather than let it use him then the special activities become a form of legalism. The individual is then just performing for an organizational process. A person needs to know what he wants to accomplish and how glorifying God will relate to his basic concerns.

ACTION

1. Assess, to the best of your ability, the personal goals and objectives of the man or woman you want to challenge to a discipleship ministry. Then try to show how they can be accomplished, at least in part, by developing this relationship with God or a multiplying~ministry. You might want to look at Chapter 1 again to get an idea of how you might approach it.
2. Make a list of the special activities you are going to use with those whom you have challenged. Of course, it is also important to list all the reasons why the activities which you have selected are going to accomplish the objectives—the objects of (1) developing your relationship with God and (2) developing a multiplying ministry. You might wish to review the examples of special activities

that were listed in this chapter before you sit down to write up your own list.

3. Challenge someone to become a multiplying disciple.

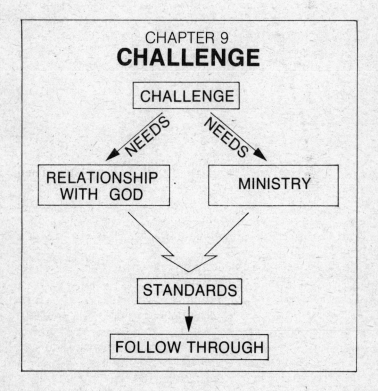

_____

_____

_____

_____
_____

PART III

THE DEVELOPMENT OF MULTIPLYING DISCIPLES

At this point in the layman's development of a multiplying-ministry he has found and challenged the men he wants to multiply through. They have been brought to this point in the environment of the four-staged following. Now, in order for them to develop as actual multiplying disciples they need to be brought into a different environment. The first environment was for preparation, but the second is for development. This environment of development takes place in the context of a small group which includes the structural group meeting as well as informal time outside the group.

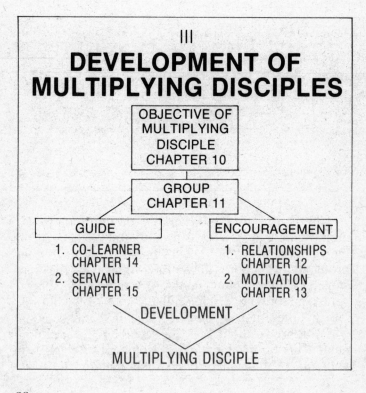

III

DEVELOPMENT OF MULTIPLYING DISCIPLES

OBJECTIVE OF MULTIPLYING DISCIPLE CHAPTER 10

GROUP CHAPTER 11

GUIDE	ENCOURAGEMENT
1. CO-LEARNER CHAPTER 14	1. RELATIONSHIPS CHAPTER 12
2. SERVANT CHAPTER 15	2. MOTIVATION CHAPTER 13

DEVELOPMENT

MULTIPLYING DISCIPLE

_____

_____

_____

_____

10.

How Do I Maintain A Vision For The World?

In this new environment that will be created for the development of the multiplying disciple it is essential that the ministry objective is always clearly seen. One must never lose sight of the world. We must also be continually reminded that multiplication through groups is our method. This chapter deals with how to help the developing multiplying disciple maintain these elements in his mind's eye.

In the second half of Chapter 2, Paul's ministry method was described as a multiplying progression through the lives of other faithful men (II Timothy 2:2). Not only was it through multiplication, it was through the multiplication of small groups. It is important to note that these groups were made up of leaders. In other words, he didn't just multiply groups of men, he multiplied groups of leaders. This was essential because those in the groups were being prepared to lead their own groups. Finally, it was observed that this method was for the purpose of reaching the world, not just a local area. The four elements in Paul's ministry were: (1) multiplication (2) the small group (3) development of leaders (4) a world objective. Simply stated, the multiplication of small groups of leaders to reach the world.

This method is difficult to put into words for the multiplying disciple to remember, so something has to be devised to keep it in his mind's eye. In Chapter 2 a picture of this process was drawn. The best way for the multiplying-disciple to remember these four elements is through that picture.

This drawing is entitled a "World Training Segment." The "World" connotes the ministry objective. "Training" contains the element of developing leadership. The ideas of the small group and multiplication are implicit in the word "Segment." The "World Training Segment" (WTS) looks like this:

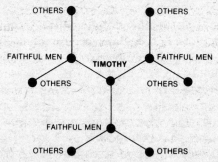

In a WTS there are actually 3 generations of individuals involved. There is the center dot—the WTS leader. Then there are 3 dots who surround the center dot, making up the second generation and finally the third generation is represented by the two dots which surround each of the dots in the second generation.

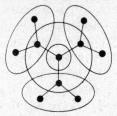

The WTS also represents 4 overlaping groupings of individuals. Each of these groupings is called a "discipler group" (this will be discussed in the next chapter) and is where much of the instruction actually takes place.

SEGMENT PICTURE IS FOR THE BENEFIT OF THE LEADER

The World Training Segment is actually for the benefit of the individual multiplying disciple. Every individual who accepts the challenge to become a multiplying disciple is given the objective to develop a World Training Segment. His objective is not to find men to disciple but instead to establish a World Training Segment. This is a very subtle but very significant concept. If an individual is challenged with finding men to disciple, he is being challenged with an addition ministry, which is quite different from a multiplication ministry.

An illustration of this was Ted. He was a man who was really interested in developing a multiplying ministry and his objective was to find men whom he could disciple. Over a period of time, Ted found a couple of other men who were interested in being discipled. They worked together for several years. They established close friendships and the other men grew in their faith. But they never really became interested in finding other men of their own to disciple.

This little group of men never did multiply because of a very simple but continually overlooked reason. They didn't have as their actual objective becoming multiplying disciples. Instead, their objective was "to be discipled" and they were in the process of accomplishing *that* objective. Ted on the other hand didn't have as his objective establishing a World Training Segment. It was, instead, to find men to disciple—which he accomplished. After Ted accomplished his objective he quit thinking in terms of his responsibility to multiplication. Ted felt if multiplication was going to take place it now depended upon Ted's men. He felt it was their responsibility not his. He had done his part.

Ted, even though he talked about building disciples, actually had an addition objective. An addition ministry is characterized by one man who reaches and builds other men but those men never reproduce other leaders. When an individual is challenged with just finding disciples, he is being challenged to a ministry of addition.

On the other hand, when an individual is challenged with a WTS he is being challenged to a ministry of multiplication. If Ted would have had an objective such as a WTS then he would have continued to feel a responsibility until multiplication had taken place. His concern would not have been just those men around him because *his* objective would have also included the men with whom *they* were working in the third generation.

Therefore, the picture of the "World Training Segment" is actually for the benefit of the multiplying disciples. It helps them understand that their objective is multiplication not addition. It is mainly for this reason that everyone who is challenged is challenged with a WTS. Each one of the three people in the second generation have as their own individual objective to establish a WTS. They each have a picture of the

WTS in which *they* are the center dot. Even the 6 third generation people on the circumference of the WTS are each challenged with their own WTS with *their* names in the center dot.

The WTS is a concept to assist the multiplying disciple in clarifying his objective. The number of dots isn't really as important as the concept. The multiplying disciple needs to be challenged with multiplication not addition..

THE WORLD TRAINING SEGMENT, A PILE OF STONES

A good scriptural illustration of the use of the WTS picture is in Joshua 4:1-7. Here God commanded the people of Israel to build a pile of stones, and He gave this reason, "Let this be a sign among you, so that when your children ask later, saying, what do these stones mean to you? Then you shall say to them, Because the waters of the Jordan were cut off before the ark of the covenant of the Lord." God used a physical picture to remind them of an important point. The pile of stones was not important in and of itself, but it was important as it caused the people of Israel to remember what God had done.

In the same way, the schematic drawing of the World Training Segment represents an objective. It is not important in and of itself but it can become important as it causes individuals to remember what their objective is so they can consciously relate all their activities to it. When the World Training Segment is used in this way, it can also be an effective instrument to help develop relational thinking.

As an illustration, Bud was a man who wanted to serve God by developing a ministry. He was very involved in Christian activity but year after year he would look back at all that activity and ask the question, "What have I really accomplished?" There did not seem to be any long-lasting effects to anything that he had done. Bud was always told as a child that "idle hands were the devil's workshop" so he had developed over the years a propensity toward activity—any type of activity. He was not so concerned with what he was accomplishing just that he was busy. Bud had managed to develop a well-entrenched terminal habit pattern of thought.

One day he went to one of his Christian meetings and was introduced to the idea of multiplication and to the concept of the World Training Segment. He reflected back on all his activity and came to the startling realization that he did not have a clear objective. He definitely had no objective to relate anything to. Bud wanted to develop a relational thinking pattern but he felt hopelessly enslaved to his terminal thinking style.

That night Bud went home and drew out a World Training Segment. Instead of drawing it out on a piece of paper though, he went to his garage and cut out a piece of plywood one foot square. He then sanded and stained the plywood a light brown. He then very carefully painted a World Training Segment on this piece of finished plywood. Every time he would paint a dot, he would pray for that disciple whom he had not met as of yet. Painting his World Training Segment was in a very real sense a prayer time for him.

After Bud had finished his World Training Segment, he took it in the house and hung it in his den. He wanted to have it in a place where it would be seen. This way everytime he saw it he was reminded to stop and think about what he was doing and then relate it to his objective. For the first time in his life Bud started to feel a sense of direction and accomplishment. He started to view his activities as a means to help him achieve his World Training Segment. Before he just viewed his activities as good things to do. Now, when Bud would attend one of his meetings he was constantly on the lookout for the men God was going to raise up. He talked to as many people as he could, looking for God's man.

It is very important to understand that the World Training Segment did not become the objective but that it represented the objective. The World Training Segment represents a multiplying ministry.

SUMMARY

In this chapter the idea of the "World Training Segment" has been introduced. By putting it in a pictorial format it helps the multiplying disciple remember that he is going to have an impact on the world through developing small groups of leaders who will multiply themselves as leaders. By remembering this he will relate all his ministry activities to the development of multiplying disciples.

ACTION

1. Build a World Training Segment on a board and put it in a place where you can see it every day.
2. Everytime you walk into the room and see it, stop and evaluate what you are doing in terms of your objective.
3. Pray for God to raise up people who will be in your "World Training Segment."

CHAPTER 10
OBJECTIVE

MULTIPLYING
DISCIPLE

↓

WORLD TRAINING
SEGMENT
PICTURE

↓

RESULTS:
- ► PERSONAL VISION
- ► RELATIONAL THINKING
- ► REACHING TO WORLD

11.

The Discipler Group

In Mark 3:13-14 it says, "And He went up to the mountain and summoned those whom He Himself wanted, and they came to Him. And He appointed twelve, that they might be with Him, and that He might send them out to preach."

WHAT DID JESUS DO?

From a following of disciples, Jesus chose His twelve. He took them out of the environment of a following into the environment of a group. Jesus used the small group method to teach and train men for an effective ministry. He gave them the priority of His time. As the time grew nearer and nearer to the cross, Jesus spent more and more time with the chosen twelve. He literally placed the responsibility of His entire ministry on a small group of men whom He discipled.

Jesus spoke to large crowds of people and He taught them from His great wisdom, but even these instances were used to give special instruction to His small group of men. For instance, in the "Parable of the Sower," Jesus tells the story of a farmer who sows seed on various types of ground. He relates the story to a large crowd who were following Him. After the story was finished, He turns to His disciples and said to them, it is granted for you to know the mysteries of the Kingdom of God, but not for the others (Luke 8:10). Jesus then proceeds to explain to His disciples the meaning of the parable. The disciples received special instruction from the Master because they were in training. They learned in a group situation and were preparing for the time when they would be the ones who would be establishing ministries.

IN THE FIRST CENTURY

The small group method of teaching and training was also used in the First Century by the apostles. In the first century, Barnabas had his small discipler group composed of Paul and John Mark. Later on, Paul established his own discipler group of Silas and Timothy. In Paul's second letter to Timothy, he challenges him to an ongoing ministry and also mentions again the method he is to use. Paul instructs Timothy to teach all that he has learned to faithful men who will in turn teach others (II Timothy 2:2).

THE DISCIPLER GROUP

We call this small group that Jesus and his apostles used the "discipler group." It is the environment where the multiplying disciple develops. Even when he leads *his* own discipler group he will continue to develop in this initial group.

It can be seen that this discipler group is one of four

in the World Training Segment.

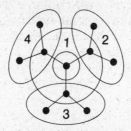

The reference in Mark 3:14 tells the two purposes of the discipler group: "be with Him"—to develop a relationship with God, and "send them out"—to develop a ministry.

In many ways the discipler group is like an island in the waters of the South Pacific. This island would be one where an environment exists which allows for the natural growth and development of plant life. The growth of palm trees would almost be a certainty. The palm trees would be of differing sizes and maturity but they would probably all produce some fruit, in the form of coconuts. The more mature a tree is, the more fruit it would probably produce.

The discipler group is an environment which has been created to encourage the natural growth and development of multiplying disciples by the work of the Holy Spirit. As these multiplying disciples develop in maturity, they produce more fruit in the form of an effective ministry and in the form of the "fruit of the Spirit." The world, represented by the salty sea, is not as conducive for the development of multiplying disciples as the environment of the discipler group, represented by the island.

The story of Henry is a good example of the importance and the advantage of the discipler group. Henry was a man who was trying to develop as a multiplying disciple without the aid of the encouraging environment of a discipler group. He realized how important it was to try new things and step out on faith so he went to a seminar at his church on how to share his faith. He went home, studied the material and then decided to try it the next day after work. Henry rode the subway home and every night he would sit next to a different person. The situation seemed perfect. One night Henry sat down next to a businessman who was reading the paper. He struck up a conversation and then launched into his presentation of the Gospel. The man with whom Henry shared was totally uninterested in the things of God and told him that only a fool would believe in all those "religious fairy tales." Henry got off the subway a discouraged man and tragically there was no one there who could talk with him and understand what he was trying to do. He tried to talk to his friend at work but he just laughed at him. Henry's friend did not believe in sharing his faith because he did not feel that people were at all interested in spiritual things. The result was that Henry never again tried to share his faith and for that matter, lost his desire completely to become a multiplying disciple.

What a difference it would have been if Henry could have related his experience to a group of close friends who were also trying to develop as multiplying disciples. They could have encouraged and reassured one another, prayed for the man on the subway or re-evaluated the method of presentation so that they could all be more effective next time. Then instead of the episode being a totally demoralizing experience, it would have been a learning and motivating time. The experience would have even drawn the discipler group members closer together as they shared common experiences and encouraged one another in their faith.

The discipler group, which is the heart of the World Training Segment, is the environment where the multiplying disciple develops in his relationship with God and his ministry. An individual, as he surveys different discipler groups, will find multiplying disciples in various stages of maturity with different rates of development. Those men and women are allowing the Holy Spirit to use the created environment to work uniquely in each of their own lives.

DISCIPLER GROUP LEADERS' PERSPECTIVE

The discipler group leader has as his objective not to just develop a discipler group but a World Training Segment. There are two basic responsibilities that an individual needs to have if he is to develop a discipler group which has as its purpose the development of a relationship with God and a multiplying ministry.

1. The first objective is to establish an atmosphere of *encouragement*. This process will be discussed in greater detail in the following chapters.
2. The second objective is to *guide* an individual in two areas: 1) his relationship with God and 2) his multiplying ministry.

For the most part, the effectiveness of the guiding or teaching elements of this process of discipleship are dependent upon the quality of environment which has been created. The encouragement acts as a channel through which the instruction and training are given.

THE DISCIPLER GROUP MEMBER'S PERSPECTIVE

The multiplying disciple who is getting involved in a discipler group should have a few necessary perspectives as he begins the developmental process.

The first perspective is that the two objectives of the discipler group—establishing a relationship with God and developing a multiplying ministry—must be his own personal objectives. He uses the discipler group to fulfill *his* objectives.

Some of the other perspectives he has is that he wants to learn not only how to develop his own relationship with God but how to teach others to effectively do the same. He wants to become independently dependent upon God. He does not want to be a man-pleaser but a God-pleaser.

This person also wants to develop his own multiplying ministry. This means that he has his own World Training Segment in which he is at the center. He does not always know whom the Lord will raise up for him to work with, but right from the beginning his objective is to establish his own World Training Segment. This person would represent one of the dots in the second generation of his discipler group leader's World Training Segment.

This person also has the perspective of using everything he learns so he will not make the same mistakes with his men. Everything is geared and related to the accomplishment of *his* purpose in life (relational thinking encouraged).

Another perspective the new multiplying disciple should have is the role and responsibility of his discipler group leader. In other words he does not look at his discipler group leader as the man with all the answers or the great Bible teacher, rather he looks at him as one who really cares about him and who really wants to see him accomplish his own objective.

SUMMARY

The World Training Segment is made up of discipler groups which are the method of giving and receiving instruction. The two purposes of the discipler group are (1) to assist those involved to develop their relationship with God and (2) to assist in developing a multiplying ministry.

Therefore, the responsibilities of the discipler group leader are primarily two in number. The first is to create an effective atmosphere of encouragement and then second, to use that atmosphere as a channel for guiding the member. These two areas of responsiblity will make it possible for the two purposes of the discipler group to be fulfilled.

ACTION

1. Consider how an atmosphere of encouragement could be developed. List the various possibilities.
2. Consider how quality teaching might be made available to the multiplying disciple if the discipler group leader is an average layman not skilled in various teaching and training techniques.

This is preparation for the discussion in later chapters.

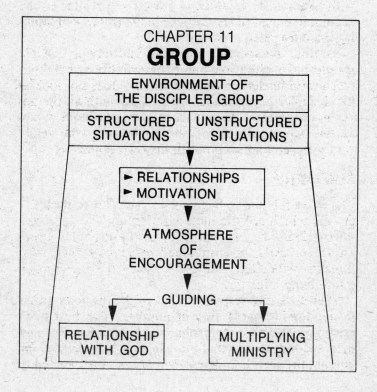

_____

_____

_____

_____

12.

Creating The Atmosphere Of Encouragement

In leading a discipler group, an individual is to create an atmosphere of encouragement and use that as a channel to instruct and teach. What is involved in creating that atmosphere? These next two chapters will discuss various aspects of that task.

WHAT DID JESUS DO?

Jesus loved the men with whom he worked. In John 15:9, Jesus states, ''Just as the Father has loved Me, I have also loved you; abide in My love.'' Love characterized the Lord's ministry.

Jesus put a high value on the quality of relationships that his disciples had with one another. He even went so far as to say that love would be the distinguishable quality which would mark men as His disciples. "By this all men will know you are my disciples, if you have love one for another" (John 13:35). Love is one of the most encouraging, motivating atmospheres for anyone's development.

IMPORTANCE OF RELATIONSHIPS

In developing a multiplying ministry of discipleship the basic structure used is the discipler group. The small group is actually the "backbone" of the multiplying ministry that is being discussed in this book and the "backbone" of the discipler group is the interpersonal relationships. If an individual cannot develop friendships with those with whom he is working he will not be able to build multiplying disciples.

Many Christians are involved in various types of ministries where it is not necessary to establish strong relationships. For instance, in a preaching ministry, an individual can be very effective without developing strong personal relationships. Other examples include intercessory prayer, driving the church bus, organizing the Father and Son Banquet, or even teaching Sunday School. These are all activities in which individuals can be involved and be relatively effective without developing strong friendships. However, it is virtually impossible to develop a discipleship ministry by the process being discussed, without the individual being able to make close friends. This method of discipleship is not based on the amount of knowledge that the discipler group leader has, but rather on his ability to recognize the man God has raised up to become his best friend.

As surveys and studies have been made across the country, the data received indicates that the effectiveness of an individual's discipleship ministry is in direct proportion to the quality of relationship he has been able to establish with his men. These studies also indicated that the personal friendships that were established were the single most important reason that people would become involved in various Christian groups.

It seems that the old adage is true which says "Who you are speaks so loudly that I can't hear what you say." Individuals followed Jesus not just because of what He said but because of who He was. He loved those to whom He ministered. He had so much compassion for people. And He accepted people just the way they were. Individuals also followed Jesus because of what He did. He did things for people. He healed their afflictions. He gave sight to the blind and He cast out the evil spirits. Jesus knew how to build relationships.

A church was sponsoring a special evangelistic outreach program for the community where the church was located. The program was to be presented on a Sunday evening during the summer. It was to be a program that the whole family could come to and the church wanted to make it as informal as possible. There would be free refreshments and an entertaining performance by a magician who would give an evangelistic message.

A special committee was created just to handle the publicity and they went "all out." The program was announced regularly on three radio stations, in the newspaper, in the local businesses via posters, and by flyers that were passed out door-to-door. There was even some television coverage.

The program was well attended and the publicity committee was very pleased but they were curious as to which one of the publicity activities was the most effective, so they took a brief survey of those that attended. What they found out was very surprising to them. Ninety percent of those that came to the performance came because someone had *personally* contacted them and asked them to come. It wasn't because of the radio spots or the newspaper ads. It was because of the personal attention that people received. This shows that people have a basic need to be accepted and to be loved as persons not just as objects to be taught and instructed. This is why relationships are so important in the development of the multiplying disciple.

INFORMAL SITUATIONS

The opportunity to minister in formal situations is an outgrowth of effective interpersonal relationships. The classroom type of environment seems to militate against quality learning and instruction. When is it that God teaches one the most in his own life? Is it in a controlled learning situation such as in a church service? Probably not. God usually teaches people the most when they do not expect it, using the great classroom of life during normal everyday activities.

Jesus almost always used this method of teaching and training His disciples. He would take an experience and use it to teach them a spiritual lesson. For instance, there was the time when Jesus and the disciples were in the boat and a violent storm came up. The disciples became terrified and Jesus calmed the storm. This experience was used to teach them about faith (Luke 4:37-40). In much the same way, when individuals spend time together, certain situations arise which the Lord can use to teach them in a manner that makes a lasting impression.

There were two men who had developed a close friendship and who were involved in the process of becoming multiplying disciples. Bill was discipling John. Every other day they would meet in a restaurant for lunch and discuss basic Christian doctrines such as forgiveness and eternal life. One day, after their usual meeting, they were walking through a downtown shopping mall jammed with people. Bill casually made the comment, "Boy, these people really need to hear about Christ." Bill was not aware of it but the Lord greatly used that comment in the life of John. Before John had given his life over to Christ, he had always been insensitive to other people's needs. He was out for all the living that he could get and unknown to Bill, John would walk across this same shopping mall, look at the crowd of people and say to himself "Look at all these stupid people." To hear Bill's words of compassion immediately brought to mind the contrast of his past attitude. God used that informal situation and the passing comment of a friend to teach John a long remembered lesson in compassion.

One of the reasons this incident had such an impact on John was because he was so unprepared for it. When he would meet with Bill in the restaurant, he expected Bill to talk about religious things, but walking through the shopping mall, John was caught completely off guard. God started to impress on him how spiritual truth could change past attitudes towards people and make him the kind of man that could glorify God with his life.

BEING REAL

Jesus continually criticized the Pharisees because they acted so religious—it was mostly just "show" for the people. In Luke 11:39, Jesus said, "Now you Pharisees clean the outside of the cup and of the platter; but inside of you, you are full of robbery and wickedness."

When an individual is involved in the discipling of another person, there is a subtle temptation to put on a "spiritual show" for that person. There are two reasons why he might do this. The first is that he desires that person to respect him as a man of God or secondly, he wants to be a good example of how a man of God should live. In any event the pressure is on to perform and to act spiritual, in other words "clean up the outside of the cup and of the platter." The result is just the opposite of what is desired—a person looks less spiritual.

Leroy and Carl are an example of this. Before the discipler group started, Leroy and Carl were pretty good friends but since Carl started discipling Leroy, their relationship had deteriorated. They used to talk about the problems they were having and how to solve them. But now Carl started to make it appear that he didn't have problems. Every time Leroy mentioned something that was bothering him, Carl responded by quoting a Bible verse and telling him that he was in sin. Carl was a sincere man of God who was trying to be a good example to the man that he was discipling. But he fell into the subtle trap of acting spiritual. A great man of God once said, "If you don't take yourself off the pedestal, God will, and it's a lot easier when you take yourself off."

God wants us to be real with those we are working with. He wants us to show them that we in ourselves are nothing but in Christ we are becoming like Him. An individual needs to be able to admit his shortcomings just as he also needs to be able to reveal his heart's desire to glorify God. God doesn't ask us to be perfect; He just wants us to love and desire Him. If the disciple with whom an individual is working is able to pick up the heart attitude of his leader, the imperfections in the personality seem less important. There is a lot of truth in the statement that "Love covers a multitude of sins."

HAVE FUN

An important aspect of being able to develop strong

relationships is having fun with those that are being built as multiplying disciples. There just does not seem to be any formal activity that can compare to good, old-fashioned fun when it comes to an effective method of developing friendships.

There are times when an individual who decides to go to the ball game with the men in his discipler group, rather than lead them in Bible Study, just may be having the more effective ministry. Relationships are built by the informal, as well as the formal times. People naturally listen to someone whom they know cares about them. A person listens to and loves to be with his friends and friends have fun together. There should be no distinctions between "ministry" and "non-ministry" time, because an individual's life *is* his ministry and his ministry is his life.

SUMMARY

An individual who is creating an atmosphere of encouragement in the discipler group needs to be able to establish strong and lasting friendships. These relationships are then used as a channel by which instruction and training can be obtained.

Jesus put a high value on interpersonal relationships and took advantage of the informal times that He had with His disciples to teach them great truths. Men who desire to establish multiplying ministries need to learn from the example that Christ has given them.

ACTION

1. Make a list of all the different informal activities in which you might be involved with those whom you are discipling.
2. Invite your disciples over for an informal dinner and discover the various areas which you might have in common.
3. Consider what "admitting your shortcomings"

and "revealing your desire to glorify God" actually means in a practical situation.

Be careful not to let the situation develop into a problem-sharing time where everyone emerges feeling defeated. That can be a very negative experience. The objective is to be able to convey that you are human just like your disciples but that more than anything else you want to glorify God with your life.

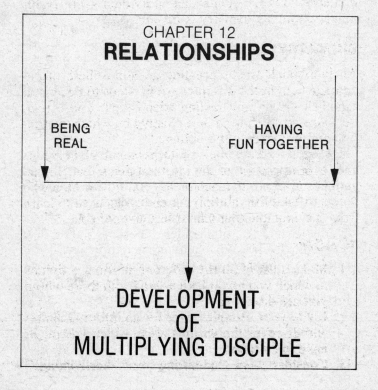

CHAPTER 12
RELATIONSHIPS

BEING
REAL

HAVING
FUN TOGETHER

DEVELOPMENT
OF
MULTIPLYING DISCIPLE

_____

_____

_____

_____
_____

13.

Developing Strengths

In creating an ATMOSPHERE OF ENCOURAGEMENT which in turn can be used as a channel to instruct and teach, it is important to add the element of motivation. Motivation is a key ingredient to the discipler group and is that elusive quality which allows an average discipler group leader to become a great discipler group leader. When a dynamic motivational atmosphere is combined with strong interpersonal relationships, an environment is created which is perfect for the Holy Spirit to use to develop each member of the discipler group at His own rate and in His own way.

In this chapter, there will be a discussion of two concepts of how to inspire motivation. Both can easily be mastered by the average person with a minimum of practice.

DEVELOPING STRENGTHS

The first concept deals with the idea of developing strengths. The first century disciples were men who had varying temperaments and personalities. For example, Peter was a man who at times exhibited quite a temper. He was a man who was outgoing and vocal. There were instances when it seemed that he would have been better off if he had kept his mouth shut and been silent. Bartholomew, on the other hand, was a man who gave the impression of being cool, calm, and collected. At times, Bartholomew, generally referred to as Nathanael, would almost seem to be detached from reality—living in a world far away from the people with whom he was involved. Then of course, there was Thomas the doubter. Here was a man who seemed to be questioning everything and anything, including the resurrection body of our Lord (John 20:26-28). He had to touch and feel the holes in the hands of the risen Christ before he would believe.

These three men are representative of the type of men that Jesus chose to be His disciples. In many ways they were not too unlike the men and women that you will select to develop as multiplying disciples. They all have unique character traits and they all have their own strengths and weaknesses.

When Jesus selected His men, he did so with the confidence of knowing what they could become. In other words, Jesus saw the potential of the men whom he had chosen.

NEGATIVE APPROACH TO STRENGTHENING

When an individual is involved in building multiplying disciples by developing an atmosphere of encouragement, there will be many times in which he works from the negatives in his multiplying disciples' lives, rather than see their potential. Illustrating this, Jane had just challenged Mary and Helen to become multiplying disciples, and they had both accepted the challenge. Jane was excited about the idea of beginning a discipler group and was beginning to create an environment by establishing good relationships with Mary and Helen. They would go shopping together, talk to each other on the phone, and pray for one another's personal needs. As time went on, Jane became closer to Mary and Helen, and differences in personalities and character traits began to become more evident.

Jane had always been a real studious person and just loved to spend hours studying the various interpretations of one verse of Scripture. Mary and Helen on the other hand, liked to read the Bible but they would get bored going over the same verse time and time again. They enjoyed activities more like visiting the nursing homes and writing letters for those who could no longer hold a pen because of age.

Jane started to become concerned. Mary and Helen were her disciples and she felt that in order for them to develop as multiplying disciples, they needed to gain personal discipline and learn to study the Scriptures the way that she did. Jane approached Mary and Helen and began to voice her concern. Every time the women would meet in their disciple group, they would study the Bible and Jane would continually point out that Helen and Mary were doing wrong. Week after week, Jane continued to focus on their weak areas in order to build them up and train them to be effective students of God's word. The only problem was that after three months, Mary and Helen came to Jane and told her that they wanted to drop out of her discipler group. They explained that they knew how important it was to study the Bible the way Jane did but they just could not do it.

In this illustration, Jane did not see Helen and Mary's potential in the area of compassion for those who were less fortunate. Instead she concentrated on their faults and their shortcomings week after week reminding them that they did not measure up. Finally, she crushed their motivation for going on completely and they dropped out of the group. Jane wanted to create a good environment in the discipler group and that is why she worked so hard at trying to build relationships. But she neglected to employ the positive perspective in motivation which is developing a person's strengths.

SELF-ESTEEM

An individual is motivated or has a sense of self-esteem when he feels that he is doing something right and is doing something that no one else is able to do.

As an illustration, there was a minister who was involved in teaching a pastor's class on how a person could know that he had eternal life. This particular class depended a lot on the interaction of the individual members. One of the main objectives of the class was to involve as many of the people as possible in the discussion, so that each person would feel a part of the whole group.

Everyone in this particular group was working in an office except for one person—Jim, a local auto mechanic. Jim felt out of place and awkward because of his occupation. As a result, he never became too involved in any of the discussions. Jim, however, had a real desire to learn about the things of God and so he continued to come every Sunday. He just didn't participate in the discussions.

One day, the minister called Jim up and asked him if he would tune up his car. Jim immediately offered his help. The minister drove right over but when he got to the garage, he stayed and watched Jim do his work. He engaged his parishioner in a conversation concerning auto mechanics and before long, he began to demonstrate his ignorance in the whole area.

The next Sunday during the pastor's class, the minister mentioned how competent and knowledgeable Jim had been, working on his car. He also explained to the class that because of Jim's particular talents and his particular sphere of influence, he would probably be able to reach people for Christ that no one else in the class could reach. Jim's self-confidence soared. He started to feel accepted—that his life had significance. He started to contribute in the class and make a stand for Christ at work. He started to work hard at developing his mechanic skills so that he could be a greater influence for Christ.

In this illustration Jim's unique skill as an auto mechanic at first was a limiting factor. He was different from the others in the class and felt inferior. Because he felt inferior, his motivation to participate was very low. The minister, however, instead of reminding Jim of the areas where he was not competent, tried to demonstrate how his uniqueness could accomplish things that others could not. The result was that Jim gained self-esteem because of the very uniqueness that, before, had caused him to feel inferior. Because Jim was developing self-esteem, his motivation level soared and it affected everything that he did—the least of which was his subsequent involvement in the pastor's class.

By encouraging and developing a person's strengths, it is possible to greatly intensify the learning environment in the discipler group. An individual will also find that the whole area of developing interpersonal relationships and close friendships will be made a lot easier because of the application of this concept. People like to be around others who think their lives have significance.

CORRECTING WEAKNESSES

Does this mean that an individual who applies the concept of developing strengths ignores his disciple's weaknesses? Never! What it does mean is that an individual's weaknesses are corrected by showing how that will make a person's strengths even more appealing.

For example, in Jane's situation, which we discussed earlier, she had two women in her discipler group who seemed to have a particular strength. Jane did not possess this strength of being able to show compassion for those less fortunate. On the other hand, Jane had a strength in the area of Bible Study discipline which Mary and Helen did not have. Jane's challenge is to emphasize Mary and Helen's strengths at the same time she develops their weaknesses. This could possibly be done by sitting down with Mary and Helen and acknowledging their particular strengths and explaining how tremendously valuable it could be in developing multiplying disciples. Then explain how developing in their personal Bible Study could make their ability to show compassion more valuable. Possibly this could be done by explaining that because of their compassion, certain people would respond with a great deal of attention. They, in turn, could use this response to teach truth from the Word if they knew how.

There will not be anyone in a discipler group alike because their strengths and weaknesses will probably be different in many respects. The general idea is to continually emphasize an individual's strengths or uniqueness, and to use them in their lives so that it would not be a demoralizing factor. Instead it would be a tremendous motivating factor which will continue to strengthen the discipler group environment.

SECOND CONCEPT

The second concept of how to inspire motivation in the discipler group deals with letting those you are leading contribute to your own life.

The apostle Paul, even before his conversion on the road to Damascus, was a very knowledgeable and intellectual man. He was considered a Pharisee of the Pharisees partly because of his specialized and intensive training as a younger man. Paul was a student of the famous Gamaliel, who was a distinguished teacher of the Law (Acts 22:3). Paul was also a Roman citizen by birth (Acts 22:28), a distinction in that time which placed him in the aristocracy class of the empire.

Barnabas, on the other hand, was a Levite by extraction and probably an early convert to Christianity. His knowledge and credentials did not compare to the great Saul of Tarsus. Yet after Paul's conversion, it was Barnabas who took Paul "under his wing" and presented him to the apostles at Jerusalem (Acts 9:27). Barnabas had created a situation because of his testimony to the apostles which allowed Paul to grow and intermingle with the other Christians. Barnabas in many ways was Paul's discipler group leader, but after working in Antioch for a time with the new church he requested Paul to assist him. Barnabas, who was the leader, was asking Paul for help.

It can be a very positive experience for the disciple to be able to contribute to his discipler's life. Not only can it become a motivating experience, it could very easily be the beginning of a lifelong friendship. The following illustration might explain the concept a little better. There was a young boy who was in the seventh grade in school. One Saturday morning, he decided to walk down to his junior high athletic field because there was supposed to be a four team invitational track meet in progress there. This boy was not really that interested in track but he thought he might see some of his friends there watching the meet. As he approached the field he searched the crowd for someone who might look familiar. This track meet like all the other junior high track meets was very informal in its program—the spectators were allowed to intermingle with the contestants.

This young seventh grader was slowly making his way through the congestion not paying the least bit of attention to what was going on when all of a sudden "out of the blue," one of the contestants turned to him and started to engage him in conversation. The boy was quite surprised for the contestant was one of the "big kids," a ninth grader and he was just a seventh grader. It so happened that the ninth grader was participating in the high jump and as the two boys talked, the contestant began to ask the younger boy for advice on what to do on his next jump. The seventh grader did not even begin to know what to say, he hardly knew what the high jump was. Then the contestant asked him, "Do you think I ought to bend a little more at the waist?" The younger boy, not knowing what else to say, said, "Yes!" It was not long until the contestant's time came to compete and he had to leave to get ready for his event.

Because of their conversation, the seventh grader's attitude changed regarding the track meet and the high jump event in particular. Where just moments before the boy had been disinterested, now he gave the high jump event his undivided attention. He watched with great enthusiasm as his new friend competed in the event.

What happened in the space of a few moments to turn the boy's apathy into intense enthusiasm? The ninth grader was secure enough in his own life to ask the boy for some advice. The boy couldn't even begin to give advice. So the ninth grader made some up and asked him to give a yes or no answer. The result was motivating and a friendship began which has lasted over twenty years.

An individual who leads a discipler group can help develop an atmosphere of encouragement and motivation by using this powerful concept. Instead of know-

ing all the answers to the problems and instead of acting like a great spiritual giant, the discipler group
leader may find it more advantageous to be himself
and ask those with whom he is working for their opinions on a particular issue. Ironically the disciple group
leader may benefit his disciples the most by letting
them teach him.

ACTION

1. Look for the strengths and weaknesses in those
   with whom you are working.
2. Try to work out a way that you can encourage the
   strengths and at the same time help them in their
   weaker areas.
3. Constantly be on the lookout for areas where
   your disciples can contribute to your life and let
   them know when they do contribute.

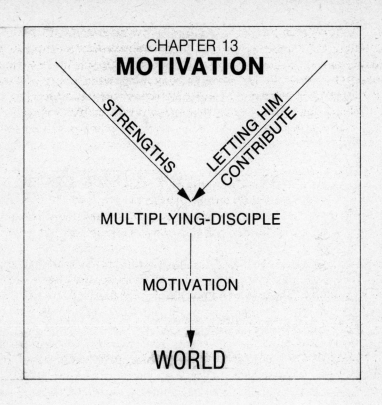

CHAPTER 13
MOTIVATION

STRENGTHS

LETTING HIM CONTRIBUTE

MULTIPLYING-DISCIPLE

MOTIVATION

WORLD

_____

_____

_____

_____

14.

The Concept
of Guiding

In leading a discipler group, the responsibilities of the leader are to create the atmosphere of encouragement and to guide his disciples as they develop in their relationship with God and their multiplying ministry. In the preceeding two chapters, the first of these responsibilities was discussed—that of creating the atmosphere of encouragement by establishing personal relationships and maintaining a motivating atmosphere. In these next two chapters an exciting, powerful concept will be discussed as the second responsibility of the discipler group leader is explored, that of guiding.

Many times there exists in a church those individuals who are faithful, have a heart for God, are teachable and get along well with people but who do not have the knowledge to teach with authority from the Scriptures. They want to be involved in building disciples but are limited by most discipleship programs. The Scripture states in Luke 6:40 that a "pupil is not above his teacher but everyone after he has been fully trained, will be like his teacher." Therefore, it is assumed that the discipler must have more spiritual knowledge and be more spiritually mature than those he is discipling. How can a man without such knowledge be involved in building disciples?

Another situation that often arises is that there are a number of relatively new and excited Christians who are full of motivation and want to be involved in the process of building multiplying disciples, but don't have the expertise needed to do so. The Scripture states not to put young believers in a position of authority (I Tim. 3:6). Therefore, it is assumed that these relatively new Christians cannot be involved in building multiplying disciples. In fact, the question is can they even be involved in the discipleship process?

Finally, the question arises as to the concept of guiding and how does it relate to the concept of building an effective environment in the discipler group?

THE CONCEPT OF GUIDING

When an individual develops as a multiplying disciple, it is realized that he develops into two main areas. As mentioned before, the first area is in his relationship with God which includes activities such as understanding the Scriptures and then applying those truths in the power of the Holy Spirit. The second area in which a multiplying disciple will develop is in his multiplying ministry which necessitates training in various ministry skills, along with principles of building a ministry. The question is how can one not competent in Biblical knowledge and ministry training skills till be able to teach those in a discipler group. The responsibility of the discipler group leader in the guiding phase is more concerned with how an individual is receiving instruction rather than the actual teaching of the material himself.

In the concept of guiding, the discipler group leader is primarily concerned with three areas: (1) rating the instruction (2) insuring that the instruction is learned and (3) that the instruction is received in a balanced way.

In rating the instruction, the discipler group leader has the responsibility of making sure that all teaching and instruction given to those in his group is good Biblical teaching. This can be done in a number of ways but possibly the most frequently used is by trusting the word of the local pastor. If the local pastor gives his approval concerning a particular conference speaker then the discipler group leader can feel confident of exposing his men to that speaker for teaching. On the other hand, if the local pastor does not give his approval then the discipler group leader should be careful not to expose his men to that teaching. The same method may be used concerning the rating of study material, books, tapes, educational films, and other sources of Biblical education or training.

The second is to insure to the best of his ability that the instruction is indeed being received. This has a lot to do with how well the atmosphere for learning has been established. Basically this responsibility deals in the area of the learner's motivation. In other words, are those in the group motivated to learn the subject matter to which the group leader exposes them? It also may be very important in this area of guiding for the discipler group leader to explore the various teaching materials available, whether it be books, tapes, Bible studies, or whatever to discover what medium his group best responds to.

The third responsibility of the discipler group leader

is to not only insure that the instruction is good and that they are indeed receiving the instruction but to try to insure that the discipler group member is receiving the instruction in a balanced way. This concept of balanced development and intake of Christian instruction has already been discussed in detail in Chapter 4.

The discipler group leader, primarily concerns himself with these three responsibilities as he leads his group. Therefore it can be seen that he doesn't need a lot of Biblical expertise in order to fulfill the guidance aspect of his responsibilities. Again, what he does is first of all *create an atmosphere of encouragement* and then he lets the Holy Spirit use the environment to teach his disciples as he "guides" them into various forms of Christian instruction.

WHO DOES THE DISCIPLING?

In I Corinthians 3:6 Paul is speaking to the church at Corinth concerning their spiritual education. He writes, "I planted, Apollos watered, but God was causing the growth." In this verse Paul was explaining to the believers that He was the one who started this church with his teaching of truth, and that many learned and became more knowledgeable as Apollos taught them truth but that the only one who caused them to actually grow was God as manifested in the Holy Spirit.

A discipler group leader who uses the guiding concept is actually encouraging the Holy Spirit to cause the growth of his disciples and consequently to develop as multiplying disciples. In this concept of guiding, the actual person who does the discipling is the Holy Spirit. The group leader merely creates a suitable environment for the Holy Spirit to work. He exposes his men to Biblical truth, but the Holy Spirit actually develops, builds, and draws out the commitment. The Holy Spirit also gives the vision for how they can become multiplying disciples.

Many times an individual may unconsciously take over and play the part of the Holy Spirit in the process of discipleship. In this case, he may feel the whole burden of growth and development in his members. In other words, he is in fact the discipler, not the Holy Spirit. He must be the one who teaches and interprets the Word to his disciples, not the Holy Spirit.

It is noted that Jesus taught and explained truth to His disciples and that His disciples did not need to go somewhere else for instruction. However, Jesus is God and it was possible for Him to answer all the questions and explain all the mysteries to the early disciples. But we are *not* God. Therefore, it is not possible in this age to give the correct answers to every question or give the perfect teaching to those in the discipler group regardless of the amount of knowledge the leader may possess. This is not to infer that a discipler group leader is not to teach. On the contrary, he is to continually develop his Biblical teaching skills. All that is being said is that the ability to develop multiplying disciples is not necessarily dependent on the leaders' ability to teach with authority from the Word. The leader is to teach those in his group but he *may* decide to teach them by exposing them to a local pastor, or someone else, who is competent in teaching with authority from the Word.

AFTER PENTECOST

In Acts 1:8, Jesus tells His disciples that they shall receive power when the Holy Spirit comes upon them and that He will enable them to be His witnesses both in Jerusalem, in all Judea and Samaria, and even to the remotest part of the earth. Then in Acts 2:4, the Holy Spirit was given in accordance with Jesus' promise. The result was that the same first century disciples who had earlier been afraid, denied Christ and doubted

His resurrection were now proclaiming Him boldly in the streets and in the market places (Acts 2:22). It was the Holy Spirit who gave the disciples their boldness and power to live and preach the Christian life.

In I Corinthians 2:12, Paul writes to the church at Corinth explaining the role of the Holy Spirit in the Christian's development. He states "Now we have received, not the spirit of the world, but the spirit who is from God, that we might know the things freely given to us by God." Paul is explaining to the believers that it is the Holy Spirit who leads them into all truth and who unveils the mysteries of God so that man might understand truth.

The first century disciples were with the Lord three years and during that time He taught them great truth and exposed them to fantastic ministry situations. But it was not until Pentecost that the disciples really did anything in the way of a ministry. It was not necessarily that the disciples needed to prepare for three years before they could have a ministry, it was the fact that they needed the power of the Holy Spirit.

A believer today has the same Holy Spirit. Therefore, he has the potential of understanding the teachings of Jesus, possibly even more readily than the first century disciples who had to wait three years for the Comforter to come. As an individual is involved in a discipler group, tremendous emphasis is always placed on the fact that it is the Holy Spirit, not the group leader, who is the actual discipler of men.

CAN YOUNG CHRISTIANS BE DISCIPLE GROUP LEADERS?

In I Timothy 3:6, the Scripture warns against putting a new convert into a position of authority in the church structure. Does this then mean that a relatively new believer cannot be a discipler group leader?

By implementing the method of developing

multiplying disciples as described in this book, it would actually be possible for the discipler group leader to be involved in developing a multiplying disciple who is more mature than himself. It is noted that in Luke 6:40, Jesus states "that a pupil is not above his teacher but everyone after he has been fully trained will be like his teacher." Because the discipler group leader is a co-learner who only creates an atmosphere and then guides, the Holy Spirit is the actual teacher. The multiplying disciple may develop beyond his discipler group leader but he will not develop above his actual teacher who is the Holy Spirit.

TWO TYPES OF DISCIPLESHIP

Often it is felt that for individuals to be ready to develop their own multiplying ministry, there needs to be a great deal of time which elapses between the moment they make a decision to have a multiplying ministry and the moment they actually begin to establish a multiplying ministry. The reason for the time lag is because it takes a great deal of instruction and training to prepare a man so that he is competent to reproduce his life in the life of another. However, with the co-learner concept it is not necessary to wait years to begin a ministry. Any individual can create an atmosphere of encouragement, guide and then learn along with those in his discipler group.

Discipleship is certainly not an instantaneous process that can be started and completed on the spot. Every individual is a unique being and the Holy Spirit develops each person as a multiplying disciple according to his own time frame. The point that is being made is that there seems to be at least two different methods of developing multiplying disciples. Both methods require the individual to develop by the Holy Spirit. Both methods require that the individual develop proficiency in Biblical knowledge and appropriate ministry training. The only major difference is in how these various requirements are satisfied.

The first and possibly more widely used method is where the discipler group leader is a knowledgeable man of the Scriptures and capable in the area of interpretation of doctrine. He might have a predetermined plan of Christian instruction which he is prepared to present to his group. This plan of Christian instruction might possibly last for years until those in the group are sufficiently trained and instructed. When that time arrives, they break out of their group and repeat the process with their own group. This process of developing multiplying disciples is very effective and great men of God are a natural result. The only limiting factors to this method of developing disciples are (1) you need a man of high qualifications to start it, (2) it takes a long time to develop potential leaders and (3) there is a tendency to become a disciple of the leader because he is so knowledgeable rather than a disciple of Christ. This, of course, is not to imply that the disciple would automatically be more willing to accept his leaders' opinions than to trust the Holy Spirit in his own life. But the tendency is there because of the overwhelming qualifications of the leaders.

The second method of developing multiplying disciples, which this book develops, is where the discipler group leader is not necessarily a man with a great amount of scriptural knowledge, but he is teachable, has a heart for God, full of the Holy Spirit, willing to develop relational thinking and demonstrates love by making friends. This man also might assemble a plan of Christian instruction which he endeavors to give to his group. But the difference is he is not necessarily teaching it. He might present the instruction by tape, film, prepared Bible Studies that his pastor gave him or by some other method. This man is a co-learner, learning along with his group. He creates an atmosphere conducive for learning and then guides and exposes his group to Christian instruction and allows the Holy Spirit to develop everyone in the group including himself. Some characteristics of this method of developing multiplying disciples are: (1) the average layman who meets the simple qualifications can be involved, (2) a great number of people can become involved right away because the discipler group leader is a co-learner, and (3) multiplying disciples are developed who are independently dependent upon God. The group cannot really depend on their discipler group leader because he is a co-learner. The tendency is more to trust the Holy Spirit in their own life. The largest limiting factor is that this method of discipleship puts a tremendous burden on acquiring the right material, tapes, etc. However, in today's society there seems to be an abundance of good Biblical study material put out by a variety of organizations. This actually can be an advantage because by exposing the discipler group to a variety of good Bible teachers, they can get a better perspective of truth than if they were exposed to just one Bible teacher.

SUMMARY

There are at least two methods of developing multiplying disciples. The objective here is not to try to prove that one is better than the other but merely to distinguish between the two. God has used both methods greatly for His glory.

ACTION

1. Make a list of the various Bible Study materials, tapes, films, etc. which are available to you.
2. From the various material, select a curriculum of instruction (perhaps your pastor can help you here.)
3. Try to discover what types of media (tapes, study material) your discipler group best responds to.

This will probably mean exposing them to a variety of things and noting which they enjoy the most.

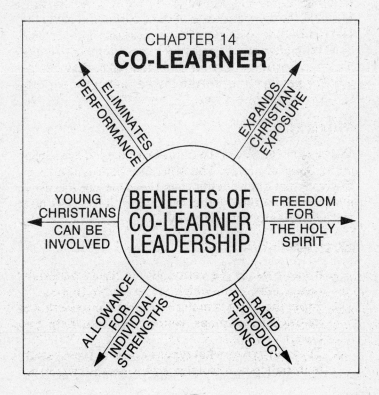

CHAPTER 14
CO-LEARNER

ELIMINATES PERFORMANCE

EXPANDS CHRISTIAN EXPOSURE

YOUNG CHRISTIANS CAN BE INVOLVED

BENEFITS OF CO-LEARNER LEADERSHIP

FREEDOM FOR THE HOLY SPIRIT

ALLOWANCE FOR INDIVIDUAL STRENGTHS

RAPID REPRODUC-TIONS

_____

_____
_____

_____
_____

15.

The Disciple As Servant

When an individual is the leader of a discipler group and is involved in the concept of guiding, he is not only a co-learner but because he is the leader, he is the servant to the others in the group. In Mark 10:43-44, Jesus spoke to His disciples and said, "but whoever wishes to become great among you shall be your servant; and whoever wishes to be first among you shall be slave of all."

The natural question which arises is, "How can you serve those in your discipler group? What can you do?" This chapter will deal with some of the things which a group leader can do to serve those in his particular group, and what the results will be.

TALKING IN TERMS OF THEIR MINISTRIES

A discipler group leader can be a servant to those in His discipler group by talking in terms of his members' ministry. Most people have a great propensity to get excited about the wrong things. Most discipleship leaders tend to get excited about what *they* are doing rather than what those in the group are doing.

As a case in point, there was a minister of a local church in the northeastern region of the United States who became very interested in developing a multiplying ministry of discipleship. He selected out of his church eight men whom he wanted to develop as multiplying disciples. This particular minister was very knowledgeable in the Word and was a very capable teacher but he decided to develop his discipler group as a co-learner. The reason that he had decided to be a co-learner was because he wanted his group to be a proto type for the groups his eight men would lead and none of them were confident enough to teach with authority.

As he worked with these eight men, he continually talked to them in terms of how they were helping *him* develop a multiplying ministry of discipleship. He never talked to them in terms of their ministries—it was always in terms of how God was using *him*.

The men came to their discipler group meetings and completed their special activities but they did not seem to have a vision for how God could use their lives. Then one day, the minister came across the verse in Mark 10 where Jesus said that to become great, a person must become a servant. He started considering how he might be a servant to his eight men and then it dawned on him that he could serve them by talking in terms of *their* ministries instead of his own. This took a little practice on the minister's part because he had never done that before. However, it was not long until he got the habit. Now instead of talking about how a

133

particular Bible study would help develop *his* discipler group, he explains how it could be used in their groups when they got theirs started. The results were dramatic. All of a sudden his eight men had their own groups and they were all using the same servant principle with the ones they were discipling.

LEARNING TO MAKE DECISIONS

A discipler group leader can be a servant to those in his discipler group as he encourages them to make more and more of their own decisions. When an individual is developing as a multiplying disciple, he also is developing as a leader—a leader who makes decisions based on his objectives and with confidence that this is the direction that the Lord would have him move. It is true that a good leader is a good follower. A good leader needs to be a close follower of Christ and needs to know how to submit to those in authority when the occasion calls for it. But to infer that a good follower is always a good leader is not necessarily true. A leader needs to be able to make decisions and he needs to be able to persuade others to follow him. If all a person can do is take orders then he will not be a good leader. A good leader must have the ability to think for himself.

For many people, the process of learning how to make decisions must be developed. All they have ever had to do to get along is do what they were told. But multiplying disciples who are being built by the Holy Spirit must be able to make their own decisions and carry through on them.

The discipler group leader can encourage this process through the role of a co-learner by continually asking discipler group members for their opinions on various subjects. The process can also be encouraged as the leader asks those in the discipler group how they are going to use the material which they have studied to establish their individual ministries.

GETTING EXCITED ABOUT
THE RIGHT THINGS

A discipler group leader can be a servant to those in his discipler group by learning to get excited about the right things. Getting excited about the right things is one of the most powerful guiding concepts that can be utilized. This concept, not unlike the principle of concentration which was discussed in Chapter III, is always in operation. It can either work for you or against you. The wise discipler group leader learns how to use this concept effectively for it can greatly affect his ministry and his life.

Basically, getting excited about the right things is a result of clear thinking and having the proper objectives. For instance, when a member of the discipler group starts talking in terms of how he thinks becoming a multiplying disciple is a good thing to do, that is one thing, but when the same discipler group member mentions how developing as a multiplying disciple is a good way to glorify God, the wise leader will go "through the roof" with excitement. The reason that the leader got excited in this particular situation is because he wanted to teach the group how to think relationally and when one of the group members demonstrated relational thinking, he got excited. By getting excited, he naturally drew attention to the importance of the issue that he wanted to teach in this case— relational thinking. People naturally like it when others get excited about what they do so the subtle tendency is for the group to think relationally.

If on the other hand, the leader does not get excited about the right things, the things he wishes to emphasize, then the principle works the other way. In the previous example, the subtle tendency would be for the group not to think relationally, if he didn't show excitement at that particular time. Getting excited about the right things can in a very real way, serve those in your discipler group and aid in the guiding process to become multiplying disciples.

ACTING AS A RESOURCE

The discipler group leader can be a servant to those in his discipler group by acting as a resource which they can use to develop their own ministry. This concept can be a very valuable asset in the guiding process of those in the discipler groups.

If the discipler group leader can convey to those in the group how they can use him to accomplish their ministries then all sorts of benefits can be seen. First of all, the group members will be lot more receptive to training and instruction because they are using it to develop their ministries. They are not just learning material because it is being offered to them. Secondly, the discipler group members will not just view themselves as being part of some type of multiplication strategy, but rather they will view themselves as *using* that strategy to accomplish their purpose in life—their purpose being to glorify God by developing their relationship with Him and by developing their multiplying ministry.

The end result is that by becoming a resource to the discipler group, the leader is becoming a servant in the true sense by assisting and encouraging the men in his group to accomplish *their* ministries.

SUMMARY

It has been shown in this chapter how (1) talking in terms of their ministries, (2) encouraging them to make decisions, (3) acting as a resource, and (4) getting excited about the right things, are all excellent methods of serving the discipler group.

ACTION

1. Begin to talk in terms of your discipler group

members' ministries.
2. List the ways you can encourage various members of your discipler group to make their own decisions.
3. List the different things you feel you can teach by the method "getting excited about the right things."

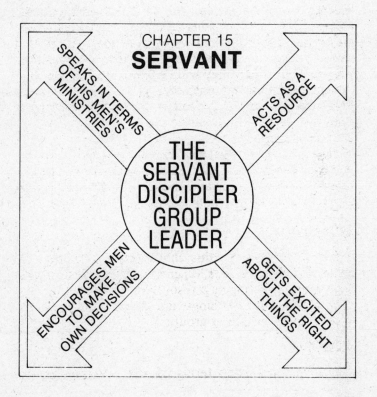

CHAPTER 15
SERVANT

SPEAKS IN TERMS OF HIS MEN'S MINISTRIES

ACTS AS A RESOURCE

THE SERVANT DISCIPLER GROUP LEADER

ENCOURAGES MEN TO MAKE OWN DECISIONS

GETS EXCITED ABOUT THE RIGHT THINGS

_____

_____

_____

_____

PART IV

DEVELOPING
A MOVEMENT

On the way to becoming a multiplying disciple it was first shown how God could greatly bless his life and how He could make an impact on the world through Him. It was then shown how to select men for his multiplying ministry, followed by the principles employed in their development.

In this section all of the elements discussed in the multiplying discipleship process are reviewed as to how they function together with one another. It will be shown then how the multiplying disciples' ministry can explode into a movement to reach the world.

DEVELOPING A MOVEMENT

MOVEMENT
CHAPTER 16

CHALLENGE
TO CHURCH
CHAPTER
17

WORLD

16.

How The Movement Grows

"Truly, truly, I say to you, he who believes in Me, the works that I do, shall he do also; and greater works than these shall he do; because I go to the Father" (John 14:12).

We have considered the thinking style of a multiplying disciple, the selection process of a multiplying disciple, and the actual development process of a multiplying disciple. The question still remaining is how can the average person expand these concepts and develop a movement through the local church to reach the world?

RELATIONSHIP BETWEEN
FOUR-STAGE FOLLOWING AND
WORLD TRAINING SEGMENT

Before an individual church can expand the discipleship concepts to develop a movement to reach the world, there needs to be a clear understanding of the relationship between the four-stage following and the world training segment. This diagram will help explain the relationship between the two.

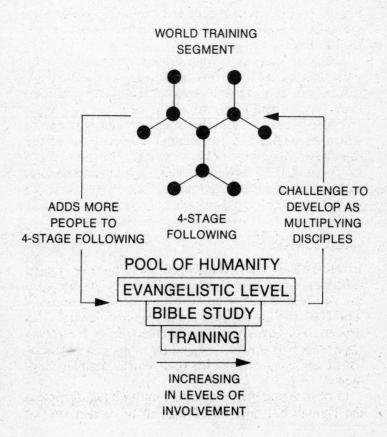

WORLD TRAINING
SEGMENT

ADDS MORE
PEOPLE TO
4-STAGE FOLLOWING

4-STAGE
FOLLOWING

CHALLENGE TO
DEVELOP AS
MULTIPLYING
DISCIPLES

POOL OF HUMANITY

EVANGELISTIC LEVEL

BIBLE STUDY

TRAINING

INCREASING
IN LEVELS OF
INVOLVEMENT

FOUR STAGE FOLLOWING

The four-stage following is an environment which is created from which to select those whom God would raise up as multiplying disciples. It consists of four stages of involvement. Each stage increases progressively in the amount of activity in which an individual participates and in his commitment to the discipleship program.

The four-stage following allows the individual to sort through his own particular situation and decide what he wants to accomplish with his life. The emphasis in this environment is for the Holy Spirit to meet a person where he is and develop him as a man of God at His own rate.

The four-stage following allows men and women with varying gifts to find the stage of involvement which best meets their own needs and to serve God in their own unique capacity. A person is not judged spiritually because of the stage of involvement in which he decides to participate. The purpose of the four-stage following is (1) to create a situation where everyone in the body can have an effective, meaningful ministry and (2) to find those whom God has raised up to be multiplying disciples.

CHALLENGE

An individual is then challenged out of the four-staged following into a discipler group where he would have the two-fold objective to (1) establish his relationship with God and (2) develop a multiplying ministry. The new multiplying disciple understands how these two objectives will glorify God and that they can be established as he establishes his own World Training Segment.

In challenging the prospective multiplying disciples, the layman has committed himself to certain special activities and a certain time commitment in order to better accomplish his objectives. These commitments are viewed as a means of keeping his life in balance as he develops and as a constant encouragement to step out in faith and try new things.

WORLD TRAINING SEGMENT

The prospective multiplying disciple will probably get involved in the World Training Segment of the person who challenged him. However, he will have as his objective to establish his own World Training Segment to help him develop a relational thinking style and a motivating vision. He understands the concept of teaching and training everyone in this World Training Segment to help them develop their own World Training Segment.

THE DISCIPLER GROUP

The discipler groups are the small groups which make up the World Training Segment. The leader of the discipler group has the responsibility to (1) create an atmosphere of encouragement and motivation and (2) to use that atmosphere to guide those involved. The atmosphere of encouragement would be created by building strong relationships and continually motivating the members. The guiding would be accomplished by the leader being a "co-learner" and becoming a servant to those in the discipler group.

The discipler group is where the multiplying disciple actually develops. He may remain in his group for as long as he wishes. Multiplication takes place as the discipler group member begins to establish his own World Training Segment by selecting his own discipler group. When a discipler group member has his own discipler group, he will then obviously belong to two groups, the one in which he is a member and the one in which he is a leader. In the group where he is a leader, he applies many of the things he learns in the group where he is a member, developing his skill of leading and developing men. In the group where he is a member, he learns new things to apply and can discuss with men in a similar situation some of the problems he is having in the group which he is leading.

ADDING MORE TO THE FOLLOWING—MAJOR PRINCIPLE

When the individual members of a discipler group begin doing the special activities to which they have committed themselves and begin to look for men whom they can challenge for their own World Training Segments, they automatically add a greater number of people to the four-staged following. For instance, as they fulfill their special activities, they will be sharing their faith regularly and will be adding people to the "pool of humanity" stage. The more people involved in the "pool of humanity," the more people there will be to filter through to the other stages of involvement and eventually become multiplying disciples. The more people who become multiplying disciples, the more people in the "pool of humanity" and so on. The result is a fast-growing, self-propagating ministry where individuals are being built and developed by the Holy Spirit.

There is a major principle of growth which this particular type of organizational development utilizes. The principle is "a movement only expands as fast as leadership is developed." In other words, there is not a continually increasing amount of activity and responsibility put on the one who started the movement. This is because the leadership is being developed that is quite capable of sharing the responsibility. In fact, the amount of responsibility which the initiator of the ministry would have could actually decrease if so desired.

145

CONTROL

A movement which has fantastic growth potential and which encourages the developing leadership to take areas of responsibility needs a method of control. This method of control will insure quality discipleship development for all who would wish to take advantage of the program in the future. What are the methods of quality control on this movement?

1. One method of control is *controlling the materials* they use in their Bible studies and action groups. The leader of a discipler group chooses the study material which he wants to use from the material that the pastor has approved.

2. Quality control can be obtained by *controlling the type of activities* used in the four-staged following.

3. Quality control can be obtained by the *type of training* used to develop the multiplying disciples in their discipler groups.

4. Another very strong and very effective method of control which is automatically involved in this particular process of discipleship is the heavy emphasis on *interpersonal relationships*. People are not rebelling and arguing with one another because they are becoming close friends.

5. *Church policies*, of course, are a way of controlling what happens.

6. The *special activities* and the *actual format* of the discipler group meeting to which those in the discipler group commit themselves is another method of control.

7. Those who actually take leadership in the four-staged following are the ones who are developing as leaders in the discipler groups. The discipler groups in turn are organized in such a way that there is a natural *chain of command* emanating from the one who began the movement. The de-

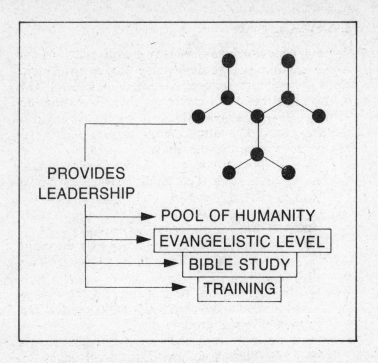

PROVIDES
LEADERSHIP

POOL OF HUMANITY

EVANGELISTIC LEVEL

BIBLE STUDY

TRAINING

veloping multiplying disciples take leadership in the four-stage following because (1) it is part of the special activities to which they have committed themselves, and (2) they are looking for men for their discipler groups. Those in the discipler groups use the four-stage following to assist them in accomplishing their personal objectives of developing their relationship with God and developing their ministry.

8. The final method of control is the *Holy Spirit* Himself. All the members of the body belong to the same Holy Spirit and God is not a God of confusion (I Corinthians 14:33). In this particular discipleship process, there is continual emphasis placed on the inner working of the Holy Spirit in the believer's life.

147

A DIAGRAM OF
HOW THE MOVEMENT GROWS

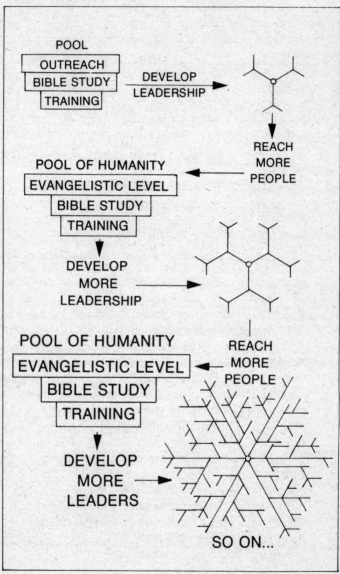

POOL
OUTREACH
BIBLE STUDY
TRAINING

DEVELOP
LEADERSHIP

REACH
MORE
PEOPLE

POOL OF HUMANITY
EVANGELISTIC LEVEL
BIBLE STUDY
TRAINING

DEVELOP
MORE
LEADERSHIP

POOL OF HUMANITY
EVANGELISTIC LEVEL
BIBLE STUDY
TRAINING

DEVELOP
MORE
LEADERS

REACH
MORE
PEOPLE

SO ON...

SUMMARY—Discipleship Paradoxes

The method of discipleship which has been presented in this book has very exciting concepts. For instance,

1. This discipleship process is very personal. Individuals establish fantastic relationships in their small discipler groups which they consider as eternal friendships.

   Yet—It is very large. This discipleship process has the potential of expanding to amazing proportions because it develops leadership—leadership which is capable of taking responsibility and proving the principle, "A movement only expands as fast as leadership is developed."

2. This discipleship process gives an individual tremendous freedom. A person involved in the four-staged following is encouraged to make up his own mind concerning what he wants to accomplish. A person is encouraged to make his own decisions and he is continually urged to allow the Holy Spirit to work out His unique plan for his life.

   Yet—It is very controlled. This process of discipleship has a tremendous amount of controlling potential. Examples are: (1) controlling the study material, (2) controlling the types of activities, (3) controlling the training, (4) controlling the policies, (5) controlling the format of the discipler group, (6) controlling through the bonds of the relationship, (7) controlling the chain of command in the discipler group strategy, and (8) control through the unifying character of the Holy Spirit.

3. This discipleship process is designed to find and develop multiplying disciples. The organization has a definite objective and is very effective in accomplishing that objective.

   Yet—A place for everyone is created. This discipleship process actually has two objectives. The first objective is developing multiplying disciples. The second is creating an environment for everyone to be involved in the body of Christ. Spirituality is not judged according to gifts; therefore, cooperation is encouraged.

4. This discipleship process produces an effective worker in the church. A man who develops as a multiplying disciple will be constantly involved in the activities of the church. He possibly could be relieving the pastor of some of his responsibilities. He is sharing Christ, bringing people to church and applying Scripture to his life in the power of the Holy Spirit.

    Yet—His objective is the world. This man has as his objective the world. He is involved in a multiplying ministry and is developing men who are able to develop others. He is involved in preparing multiplying disciples who are capable of developing their own World Training Segment wherever they might be.

5. This discipleship process emphasizes a well-organized procedure. The activities in the four-staged following, as well as the four-staged following itself, is well organized, considering the increasing stages of involvement. The discipler group is well-organized in a neat chain of command and the meeting itself is outlined very clearly.

    Yet—It depends on the Holy Spirit. The organization of the four-stage following is only effective as the Holy Spirit moves a person through the stages of involvement. Even the discipler group is dependent on the Holy Spirit to be the one who actually does the discipling as the co-learner concept is applied.

6. The discipleship process has two definite objectives—the first is to find and select a

multiplying disciple. The second objective is to actually develop the multiplying disciple in the power of the Holy Spirit.

Yet—It is used to accomplish personal objectives. The individual is encouraged to develop his own goals. He views the four-stage following and discipler group as tools for him to use.

7. The discipleship process has a definite procedure. An individual approaches discipleship with a particular mind-set—that of using the organization instead of letting the organization use him. He becomes involved in the stages of involvement. Finally, he is involved in a discipler group with a particular schedule of procedure.

Yet—It produces a man who is independently dependent upon God. An individual who develops in the context of a discipler group is constantly encouraged to develop a relational thinking style. He becomes a man who knows what he wants to accomplish and is capable of developing his own method of accomplishing it. He is independent of other men, but dependent upon God.

8. The discipleship process can be used to develop effective multiplying disciples. When an individual has gone through the discipleship process he understands how to maintain a balance in his own life and how to train others to do the same. He has had experience in challenging and selecting men for development. He has a vision, a philosophy and an understanding of how to use his life in unbelievable ways for the glory of God.

Yet—It produces leadership for the World. The world today needs men in government and other positions of authority who have developed a powerful relational thinking style. The world is ready to follow committed men who know where they are going. A man who develops as a multiplying disciple by the process described in this book also develops leadership skills which can definitely be used in our society at large.

9. The discipleship process allows an individual to be well-trained and developed. Each person is trained in knowledge and application of Biblical truth. He is trained in ministry techniques, how to develop relationships, lead small groups, challenge others, and how to depend upon the power of the Holy Spirit. He is developed in all these areas in a balanced way.

Yet—The average layman can be involved in doing it. Through the application of the various concepts such as the "co-learner," creating the environment, guiding and developing motivation, the average man can be involved in the development of a fantastic multiplication ministry. The only qualifications that he needs are: (1) a heart for God, (2) a teachable attitude, (3) a willingness to develop relational thinking, (4) the ability to demonstrate love by making friends and (5) moment-by-moment dependence on the power of the Holy Spirit.

_____

_____

_____

_____

17.

The Role
Of The Church

The church in today's world has an almost staggering
potential of increasing in its effectiveness. Three main
implications are discussed in this chapter. The first
deals with the church in our mobile society. The second deals with the church in the community, and the
third deals with the church becoming a leadership potential for the World.

IN THE MOBILE SOCIETY

We have seen that the Great Commission is God's
Goal (Matthew 28:19, 20). God's method to reach His
goal is the process of multiplication (II Timothy 2:2)

through the power of the Holy Spirit (Ephesians 5:18). How can the local church have a significant part in this building and maintaining of a multiplying ministry to reach the World?

There are at least two possible approaches in which the local church can propagate multiplying disciples in all parts of the nation and the world. The first method is much like the apostle Paul's ministry. A believer would leave home, go into another town, probably many miles away, and work with those people for a couple of years until they are to the point where they can guide themselves. This would include, being able to teach themselves from the Word, share their faith effectively with their neighbors and to develop spiritual maturity. After the people in this new town were capable of continuing on with the Lord by themselves, the believer who started the work would move on to the next town and repeat the same process.

The major problem today with this method is that most of the believers in a congregation are not in a position to "pull up stakes" and move to another town every two years or so. They have to take into consideration the children in school, their present job, the mortgage on the house and a host of other responsibilities which are important if they are to glorify God in the situation He has placed them in at the moment.

The second approach would be to train those that God has placed around the local congregation. Then instead of the believer himself going to these other cities, he trains those believers around him to be multiplying disciples so that when they move to another town—because of a job transfer or whatever—they would be fully equipped to establish the same type of multiplying ministry. Therefore, the leader wouldn't have to leave.

The significance of this second approach might be better appreciated by a conversation between a water company official of a large metropolitan city which had a population of approximately 750,000 people and a friend of his. He was asked how many new water meters his men put into homes every month. He responded that his men turned on or put in an average of five to six thousand meters per month or about 60,000 per year. Each water meter that is turned on or put in represented a family that was moving. They may be moving across town or they may be moving to or from another city.

A prominent real estate broker discovered that the average married couple between the ages of 25 and 40 move an average of once every three years. This real estate broker's business was set up with these statistics in mind.

The church today is living in a mobile society. Families are crisscrossing the United States and even moving to foreign countries in fantastic numbers. Think of the fantastic world impact the church can have if it educates and trains its people to have a multiplying ministry to reach the world. The church becomes a training center to fulfill the Great Commission by training men and women in their faith and then equipping them to establish a multiplying ministry wherever God might send them. These people would be a new type of missionary. Ones which the local church does not need to support financially but who instead actually support the local church from their individual secular occupations.

WORLD TRAINING CHURCH

The World Training Church is defined as the church that equips multiplying disciples to go to the world. This new type of church does not just have programs but is developing a dynamic, organized, living movement of God. This movement would use many of the principles discussed in this book to produce the greatest amount of trained leadership or multiplying disciples to go to the World.

WINNING

The World Training Church would have a continual and natural evangelization thrust in the local community, exposing residents to the gospel on a regular basis. This would be necessary in order for the members of church to find those whom God has raised up to be developed as multiplying disciples. Evangelism is also a means that God uses to keep believers fresh in their walk with Him—a quality which is certainly important if an individual is to be built into a leader. Finally evangelistic outreach provides a continual opportunity for the church to expose the developing multiplying disciples to the practical ministry situations in which he is being trained.

BUILDING

The World Training Church would be involved in building those that God has raised up by creating an environment which is conducive for the work of the Holy Spirit. Those who would be developing as multiplying disciples would be able to grow in their faith by gathering knowledge about the Bible and the ministry of the Holy Spirit. They also would be exposed to various ministry situations which would give them an opportunity to apply their knowledge. The World Training Church would equip its members with tools to use so they could teach their faith effectively when they were placed in new ministry situations.

SENDING

The World Training Church would be involved in sending those multiplying disciples throughout the world as God, in His timing, allowed job transfers and other such circumstances to place people in strategic cities all over the world. These people would be equipped with a tested knowledge of their faith. They would have a vision for reaching the world and they would know that God could use their life in a dynamic way. They would have developed a powerful relational thinking style which would put them in high esteem with their peers. These multiplying disciples would know how to start, build and maintain an effective multiplying ministry wherever they go because they would have had the practical experience as God had already used them in their own community.

The church is in a strategic position in a mobile society. It can find and develop multiplying disciples to go to the world. The church can have a world-wide impact.

IN THE COMMUNITY

The local church already represents the focal point of unified worship in the community. As this program of multiplying discipleship is implemented, the local church could possibly increase its role to literally become the heartbeat of community life.

SUCCESS IN LIFE

An individual who begins to develop as a multiplying-disciple usually does so because he realizes that that is the most effective way to establish a vital, ongoing, relationship with God and a dynamic multiplication ministry. He also realizes that establishing his relationship with God results in the most abundant life possible. He looks at spiritual maturity as having a definite and direct relationship to his life in the everyday world outside the church. He understands how spiritual maturity could affect his job as his character developed, how it would develop his marriage as leadership traits emerged, how his relationship with the children would be effected as his priorities fell in order and how his life in general would develop a positive attitude. He might have understood these things before but now he has committed a time segment of his life to develop these areas in reality. He has demonstrated that commitment by accepting the challenge to become a multiplying disciple. The activities that he uses to become a multiplying disciple are primarily those activities offered by the local church. Therefore, the local church becomes more than a symbol of unified worship, it becomes the vital ingredient to success in his life.

When an individual develops as a multiplying disciple, he also realizes the fantastic significance of establishing a multiplying ministry. He increasingly understands how God can use his life in undreamed of ways and how his life can really count for good in today's world. Now it is possible through the process of multiplication to actually affect the lives of people on the other side of the world. The individual who is developing as a multiplying disciple views his local church as that instrument of God which has been used to give him self-worth. Since the activities to help an individual become a multiplying disciple are offered through the church, the church is viewed as a means to establish a dynamic purpose for life.

DEVELOPMENT OF RELATIONAL THINKING

The fantastic potential of relational thinking has already been discussed. As an individual develops as a multiplying disciple by applying these principles through the power of the Holy Spirit he also develops a thinking style that will produce a dynamic motivating vision. The individual views the church as the instrument God is using to unleash that dynamic, "self-starting" force within his life. As he is involved in the multiplying discipleship program of the church, possibly for the first time the individual is able to experience the transformation by a renewing of the mind which is presented in Romans 12:1-2.

EMPHASIS ON
THE DEVELOPMENT OF GIFTS

The local church which implements a multiplying discipleship program will put a tremendous emphasis on the development of gifts and ministries other than discipleship. That church will show how the body can work together in unity and harmony. There will be a tremendous emphasis on the establishment of interpersonal relationships and an appreciation for the uniqueness of the individual.

In summary, the church becomes the place where an individual can best develop in every area of his life. The church will be the center of community life.

AS A POTENTIAL FOR WORLD LEADERSHIP

There is a tremendous leadership gap in the world today. People are generally apathetic about everything except their own selfish desires. Never before has there been such a dramatic opportunity for the local church. By implementing a discipleship process similar to the one described in this book the church can actually become the only place in the United States where responsible, developed leaders are consistently being produced. For instance, when a person is built by the Holy Spirit in the context of a multiplying discipleship process, many leadership qualities are developed such as (1) relational thinking (2) the ability to plan and organize, (3) the ability to develop relationships and (4) the ability to develop character.

RELATIONAL THINKING

Relational thinking has already been discussed in detail in the many previous sections, but it is important to draw attention to it again as it relates to the characteristics of great leaders. An individual who is able to develop this fantastic thinking style is a dynamic self-motivator. He knows what he wants to accomplish and how to do it. He has a vision of how God can use his life and a definite commitment to that end. In a world where most of the population is apathetic, a man who is committed and ready to die for his beliefs stands out and naturally attracts a following.

LEARNS TO MOTIVATE

When an individual develops in this process of multiplying discipleship, he learns to challenge, to create an effective environment and to motivate others to accomplish objectives. This skill of motivating is one of the most valuable skills an effective leader has and he will use it often.

PLAN, ORGANIZE AND CONTROL

An individual who develops his own World Training Segment must learn to plan his activities and his own method of accomplishing his objectives. He must learn to organize in such a way that his efforts do not conflict with what others are doing. Therefore he learns how to use existing programs and how to organize his time to get the most out of them. He must also learn how to control—how to keep things from getting out of hand yet maintain the right principles of control. These are the qualities of one who is a leader.

DEVELOP CHARACTER

As an individual develops in his relationship with God, he is developing his character in the most effective way possible. He becomes a man who is not a man-pleaser but who is responsible and is dependent on God. He is a man who understands what is involved in

160

applying truth to his life in the power of the Holy Spirit. He is a man with a dynamic inner strength which easily manifests itself in a society of insecure, self-adulating people. Therefore the church could be the place where the leaders for government, business, television, and so on are developed. The committed Christians would then be the ones in the influential positions of our country.

SUMMARY

The church, in implementing this program of developing multiplying disciples, can thus assert itself in the world by having an influence completely out of proportion to its size. It can literally affect millions all over the world for the cause of Christ.

The church can also become the focal point of the community as men and women see how their personal hopes and dreams can be achieved through dedicated involvement.

Finally, the church can be the new source of leadership in the world today. It is actually one of the very few places where an individual is encouraged to develop leadership skills.

The local church can actually have an impact on the society in which we live in a dramatic way that has not been seen since the First Century. The average layman in God's church would once again be accused of "turning the world upside down."

APPENDIX

_____

_____

_____

_____
_____

1.

POSSIBLE TOPICS FOR WORLD TRAINING SEGMENT CURRICULUM

PERSONAL LIFE
Bible Study Methods
Book Studies and Topical Studies
Personal Management Principles: setting personal objectives, making weekly schedules, developing relational thinking
Devotional Life
Prayer
God's Will and Servanthood
Spirit-filled Life
Christian Fellowship

Meditation on Scripture
Self-acceptance
Christian View of Finances
Dating
Quiet Time
Handling Problems and Disappointments
Application of Scripture

MINISTRY LIFE
Philosophy and Vision for Multiplication: World
Training Segment
Evangelism Tools, Follow-up Tools, Discipleship
Tools
Evangelism Skills with Individuals and Groups
Follow-up Skills
Leading Small Groups
Principles for Motivation
Management Skills—organizing, planning, writing objectives
Development of Personal Vision

_____

_____

_____

_____

_____

2.

PREPARATION GUIDE FOR DISCIPLER GROUP MEETINGS

Write clear, specific, measurable

1. What Biblical truths or principles do I want to discuss?

TIME	EMPHASIS
15 to 60 min.	ESTABLISH THE ATMOSPHERE

bjectives for your meeting.

2. What ministry skill do the group members need to learn and use?

GUIDANCE POINTS	POSSIBLE METHODS
Purpose: to establish an atmosphere of open communication among the members. How can you set an informal tone—a place where the members feel comfortable with each other?	• Eat a meal together. • Sing a few songs. • Share what God has been doing recently.

30 to 60 min.

**DEVELOP PERSONAL
GROWTH THROUGH
BIBLICAL TRUTHS**

30 to 60 min.

**DEVELOP TRAINING
THROUGH TEACHING
MINISTRY SKILLS**

Purpose: to share Biblical truths in order that personal application of the truths will be made to each member's life.

Time for study or explanation of the Scriptures and time for application of the truths to life.

Ask members: How does the Holy Spirit relate to this?
How would you apply that to your life?

Ask yourself: Do these questions keep the discussion practical? Will this Bible study meet their needs? Have the questions moved to real-life situations and experiences?

- Work through already prepared Bible study material
- Leader's own personal material.
- Pastor's own Bible study material.
- Listen to tapes or see films.
- Discussion of personal Bible study completed during the week.
- Use questions and answers.
- Give assignments.
- Discuss what God is teaching you.

Purpose: to learn knowledge and skills that will help members establish their own ministries.
Possible topics to cover: how to share your faith, how to write and give a testimony, how to lead a Bible study, how to follow up a new Christian.

Maintain the role of a co-learner. Talk in terms of the member's personal lives and ministries. Discuss how and when they can use their new skill.

- Give reading assignments.

- Role play the skill in a classroom setting with the other members.

- Plan a field experience using the new skill.

3.
PREPARATION WORKSHEET
FOR A
DISCIPLER GROUP MEETING

OBJECTIVES	EMPHASIS
	ESTABLISH THE ATMOSPHERE
	DEVELOP PERSONAL GROWTH THROUGH BIBLICAL TRUTHS
	DEVELOP TRAINING THROUGH TEACHING MINISTRY SKILLS

WHAT WILL YOU DO/SAY	WHAT WILL MEMBERS DO/SAY

*Note you will probably need to use more paper for your material.

_____

_____

_____

_____

_____

4.

QUESTIONS TO ASK AFTER PREPARING EACH MEETING

1. Are the topics I am discussing based on subjects the members need to help them grow?
2. Have I kept a balance between knowledge and application in each of the areas?
3. Am I giving equal time to getting into the Bible and learning ministry skills?
4. Are the members applying the knowledge to their lives?
5. Am I going over a predetermined course of study which is not based on the member's needs?

ACTION

1. Prepare some material you might want to use in the personal growth section of a discipler group meeting. Your pastor could probably recommend something.
2. Prepare some material you want to use in the training section. Your pastor may help here also.
3. Prepare a discipler group meeting, using the guide and worksheet. Plan content based on the particular needs and situations of your members.

If you have a hard time finding good material for Part II and III of the discipler group, write to Campus Crusade for Christ. They have an abundance of top quality material that you could use.